Managing
in the
Next Society

MANAGING

IN THE NEXT SOCIETY

Peter F. Drucker

T·T

TRUMAN TALLEY BOOKS
ST. MARTIN'S PRESS
NEW YORK

www.stmartins.com

The articles included in this book have been previously published in slightly different form. See the Acknowledgments on pages 301–303, which constitute a continuation of this copyright page.

Illustration by Adam Niklewicz

Library of Congress Cataloging-in-Publication Data

Drucker, Peter Ferdinand.
    Managing in the next society / Peter F. Drucker.
      p.   cm.
    "Truman Talley Books."
    ISBN 0-312-28977-4
    1. Management.   2. Industrial management.   I. Title.

HD31 .D77339 2002
658—dc21

                                 2001054096

First Edition: July 2002

10 9 8 7 6 5 4 3 2 1

Contents

Preface

I did once believe in a New Economy. The year was 1929 and I was a trainee in the European headquarters of a major Wall Street firm. My boss, the firm's European economist, was convinced that the Wall Street boom would go on forever; he wrote a brilliant book entitled *Investment* to prove "conclusively" that buying American common stock was the one absolutely foolproof way to get rich quick. Being the firm's youngest trainee—I was not yet twenty—I was recruited to be my boss's research assistant, the book's proofreader, and its index-maker. The book was published two days before the New York stock market crash and disappeared without a trace—and a few days later, so did my job.

And so, when seventy years later, in the mid-1990s,

there was all that talk of the New Economy and of a perpetual stock market boom, I had been there before. The terms that the 1990s used were, of course, different from those of the 1920s—we then talked of "perpetual prosperity" rather than a New Economy. But only the terms were different; everything else, the arguments, the logic, the predictions, the rhetoric, was practically the same.

But at the time when everyone began to talk of the New Economy, I became aware that Society *was* changing, and more and more so as the decade progressed. It was changing fundamentally and not only in the developed countries, but in the emerging ones perhaps even more. The Information Revolution was only one factor, and perhaps not even the most potent one. Demographics were at least as important, especially the steadily falling birthrates in the developed and emerging countries with a resulting fast shrinkage in the number and proportion of younger people and in the rate of family formation. And while the Information Revolution was but the culmination of a trend that had been running for more than a century, the shrinkage of the young population was a total reversal and unprecedented. But there is also another total reversal, the steady decline of manufacturing as a provider of wealth and jobs to the point where, economically, manufacturing is becoming marginal in developed countries but, at the same time, in a seeming paradox, politically all the more powerful. There is—again unprecedented—the transformation of the workforce and its splintering.

These changes, together with the social impacts of the

Information Revolution, are the main themes of this book—and these changes have already happened. Irreversibly, the Next Society is already here.

Some of the chapters in this book deal with traditional "management" topics, some do not. And none deals with the "cure-alls," the assertedly "infallible" tools and techniques that provided much of the substance for so many of the management bestsellers of the 1980s and 1990s. Yet this is very much a book for executives and indeed very much a book about managing. For the thesis that underlies all the book's chapters is that major social changes that are creating the Next Society will dominate the executive's task in the next ten or fifteen years—maybe even longer. They will be the major threats and the major opportunities for every organization, large or small, business or nonprofit, American—North and South, European, Asian, Australian. Indeed it is the thesis underlying every chapter of this book that the social changes may be more important for the success or failure of an organization and its executives than economic events.

For half a century, from 1950 to the 1990s, enterprises in the free, noncommunist world and their executives could and did take society very much for granted. There were rapid and profound economic and technological changes. But society was very much a given. Economic and technological changes will surely continue. Indeed the concluding pages of this book—the section "The Way

Ahead" in Part IV—argues that major new technologies are still ahead of us, and that most of them, with high probability, will have nothing or little to do with information. But to be able to exploit these changes as opportunities for the enterprise—again, for both businesses and nonprofits, whether large or small—executives will have to understand the realities of the Next Society and will have to base their policies and strategies on them.

To help them do this, to help them successfully manage in the Next Society, is the purpose of this book.

All the chapters in this book were written before the terrorist attacks on America in September of 2001. All but two of them (chapters 8 and 15) were actually published before September 2001* and no attempt has been made to update the chapters. Except for a few small cuts and corrections of typographical and spelling errors (and, in a few cases, changing the title back to my original title) each chapter is being published as it originally appeared. This means, specifically, that "three years ago" in a chapter first published in 1999 refers to the year 1996; a sentence in the same chapter reading "three years hence" refers to the year 2002. This will also enable the reader to judge whether this author's anticipations and forecasts came true or were disproven by events.

The terrorist attacks of September 2001 should make

---

*The year of first publication is shown at the end of each chapter.

this book even more relevant to the executive, and even more timely. Terrorists and America's response to them have profoundly changed world politics. We clearly face years of world disorder, especially in the Mideast. But in a period of unrest and rapid changes such as we surely face, one cannot successfully manage by being clever. Management of an institution, whether a business, a university, a hospital, has to be grounded in basic and predictable trends that persist regardless of today's headlines. It has to exploit these trends as opportunities. And these basic trends are the emergence of the Next Society and its new, and unprecedented, characteristics, especially the global shrinking of the young population and the emergence of the new workforce; the steady decline of manufacturing as a producer of wealth and jobs; and the changes in the form, the structure, and the function of the corporation and of its top management. In times of great uncertainty and unpredictable surprises, even basing one's strategy and one's policies on these unchanging and basic trends does not automatically mean success. But not to do so guarantees failure.

Peter F. Drucker
Claremont, California
Easter 2002

Part I

THE INFORMATION SOCIETY

1

Beyond the Information Revolution

The truly revolutionary impact of the Information Revolution is just beginning to be felt. But it is not "information" that fuels this impact. It is not "artificial intelligence." It is not the effect of computers and data processing on decision-making, policymaking, or strategy. It is something that practically no one foresaw or, indeed, even talked about ten or fifteen years ago: *e-commerce*—that is, the explosive emergence of the Internet as a major, perhaps eventually *the* major, worldwide distribution channel for goods, for services, and, surprisingly, for managerial and professional jobs. This is profoundly changing economies, markets, and industry structures; products and services and their flow; consumer segmentation, consumer

3

values, and consumer behavior; jobs and labor markets. But the impact may be even greater on societies and politics and, above all, on the way we see the world and ourselves in it.

At the same time, new and unexpected industries will no doubt emerge, and fast. One is already here: biotechnology. And another: fish farming. Within the next fifty years fish farming may change us from hunters and gatherers on the seas into "marine pastoralists"—just as a similar innovation some ten thousand years ago changed our ancestors from hunters and gatherers on the land into agriculturists and pastoralists.

It is likely that other new technologies will appear suddenly, leading to major new industries. What they may be is impossible even to guess at. But it is highly probable— indeed, nearly certain—that they will emerge, and fairly soon. And it is nearly certain that few of them—and few industries based on them—will come out of computer and information technology. Like biotechnology and fish farming, each will emerge from its own unique and unexpected technology.

Of course, these are only predictions. But they are made on the assumption that the Information Revolution will evolve as several earlier technology-based "revolutions" have evolved over the past five hundred years, since Gutenberg's printing revolution, around 1455. In particular the assumption is that the Information Revolution will be like the Industrial Revolution of the late eighteenth and early nineteenth centuries. And that is indeed exactly how the Information Revolution has been during its first fifty years.

The Railroad

The Information Revolution is now at the point at which the Industrial Revolution was in the early 1820s, about forty years after James Watt's improved steam engine (first installed in 1776) was first applied, in 1785, to an industrial operation—the spinning of cotton. And the steam engine was to the first Industrial Revolution what the computer has been to the Information Revolution—its trigger, but above all its symbol. Almost everybody today believes that nothing in economic history has ever moved as fast as, or had a greater impact than, the Information Revolution. But the Industrial Revolution moved at least as fast in the same time span and had probably an equal impact if not a greater one. In short order it mechanized the great majority of manufacturing processes, beginning with the production of the most important industrial commodity of the eighteenth and early nineteenth centuries: textiles. Moore's Law asserts that the price of the Information Revolution's basic element, the microchip, drops by 50 percent every eighteen months. The same was true of the products whose manufacture was mechanized by the first Industrial Revolution. The price of cotton textiles fell by 90 percent in the fifty years spanning the start of the eighteenth century. The production of cotton textiles increased at least 150-fold in Britain alone in the same period. And although textiles were the most visible product of its early years, the Industrial Revolution mechanized the production of practically all other major goods, such as paper, glass, leather, and bricks. Its impact was by no means confined to consumer goods. The production of iron and ironware—for example, wire—became mechanized and steam-driven as fast as did that of textiles, with the same effects on cost, price, and output. By the end of the Napoleonic Wars the making of guns was steam-driven throughout Europe; cannons were made ten to twenty times as fast as before, and their cost dropped by more than two-thirds. By that time Eli Whitney had similarly mechanized the manufacture of muskets in America and had created the first mass-production industry.

These forty or fifty years gave rise to the factory and the "working class." Both were still so few in number in the mid-1820s, even in England, as to be statistically insignificant. But psychologically they had come to dominate (and soon would politically also). Before there were factories in America, Alexander Hamilton foresaw an industrialized country in his 1791 *Report on Manufactures*. A decade later, in 1803, a French economist, Jean-Baptiste Say, saw that the Industrial Revolution had changed economics by creating the "entrepreneur."

The social consequences went far beyond factory and working class. As the historian Paul Johnson has pointed out, in *A History of the American People* (1997), it was the explosive growth of the steam-engine-based textile industry that revived slavery. Considered to be practically dead by the Founders of the American Republic, slavery roared back to life as the cotton gin—soon steam-driven—created a huge demand for low-cost labor and made breeding slaves America's most profitable industry for some decades.

The Industrial Revolution also had a great impact on the family. The nuclear family had long been the unit of production. On the farm and in the artisan's workshop, husband, wife, and children worked together. The factory, almost for the first time in history, took worker and work out of the home and moved them into the workplace, leaving family members behind—whether spouses of adult factory workers or, especially in the early stages, parents of child factory workers.

Indeed, the "crisis of the family" did not begin after the Second World War. It began with the Industrial Revolution—and was in fact a stock concern of those who opposed the Industrial Revolution and the factory system. (The best description of the divorce of work and family, and of its effect on both, is probably Charles Dickens's 1854 novel *Hard Times*.)

But despite all these effects, the Industrial Revolution in its first half century only mechanized the production of goods that had been in existence all along. It tremendously increased output and tremendously decreased cost. It created both consumers and consumer products. But the products themselves had been around all along. And products made in the new factories differed from traditional products only in that they were uniform, with fewer defects than existed in products made by any but the top craftsmen of earlier periods.

There was only one important exception, one new product, in those first fifty years: the steamboat, first made practical by Robert Fulton in 1807. It had little impact until thirty or forty years later. In fact, until almost the end of the nineteenth century more freight was carried on the world's oceans by sailing vessels than by steamships.

Then, in 1829, came the railroad, a product truly without precedent, and it forever changed economy, society, and politics.

In retrospect it is difficult to imagine why the invention of the railroad took so long. Rails to move carts had been around in coal mines for a very long time. What could be more obvious than to put a steam engine on a cart to drive it, rather than have it pushed by people or pulled by horses? But the railroad did not emerge from the cart in the mines. It was developed quite independently. And it was not intended to carry freight. On the contrary, for a long time it was seen only as a way to carry people. Railroads became freight carriers thirty years later, in America. (In fact, as late as the 1870s and 1880s the British engineers who were hired to build the railroads of newly westernized Japan designed them to carry passengers— and to this day Japanese railroads are not equipped to carry freight.) But until the first railroad actually began to operate, it was virtually unanticipated.

8

Within five years, however, the Western world was engulfed by the biggest boom history had ever seen—the railroad boom. Punctuated by the most spectacular busts in economic history, the boom continued in Europe for thirty years, until the late 1850s, by which time most of today's major railroads had been built. In the United States it continued for another thirty years, and in outlying areas—Argentina, Brazil, Asian Russia, China—until the First World War.

The railroad was the truly revolutionary element of the Industrial Revolution, for not only did it create a new economic dimension but also it rapidly changed what I would call the *mental geography*. For the first time in history human beings had true mobility. For the first time the horizons of ordinary people expanded. Contemporaries immediately realized that a fundamental change in mentality had occurred. (A good account of this can be found in what is surely the best portrayal of the Industrial Revolution's society in transition, George Eliot's 1871 novel, *Middlemarch*.) As the great French historian Fernand Braudel pointed out in his last major work, *The Identity of France* (1986), it was the railroad that made France into one nation and one culture. It had previously been a congeries of self-contained regions, held together only politically. And the role of the railroad in creating the American West is, of course, a commonplace in U.S. history.

Routinization

Like the Industrial Revolution two centuries ago, the Information Revolution so far—that is, since the first computers, in the mid-1940s—has only transformed processes that were here all along. In fact, the real impact of the Information Revolution has not been in the form of "information" at all. Almost none of the effects of information envisaged forty years ago have actually happened. For instance, there has been practically no change in the way major decisions are made in business or government. But the Information Revolution has routinized traditional *processes* in an untold number of areas.

The software for tuning a piano converts a process that traditionally took three hours into one that takes twenty minutes. There is software for payrolls, for inventory control, for delivery schedules, and for all the other routine processes of a business. Drawing the inside arrangements of a major building (heating, water supply, sewerage, and so on) such as a prison or a hospital formerly took, say, twenty-five highly skilled draftsmen up to fifty days; now there is a program that enables one draftsman to do the job in a couple of days, at a tiny fraction of the cost. There is software to help people do their tax returns and software that teaches hospital residents how to take out a gallbladder. The people who now speculate in the stock market on-line do exactly what their predecessors in the 1920s did while spending hours each day in a brokerage office.

The processes have not been changed at all. They have been routinized, step by step, with a tremendous saving in time and, often, in cost.

The psychological impact of the Information Revolution, like that of the Industrial Revolution, has been enormous. It has perhaps been greatest on the way in which young children learn. Beginning at age four (and often earlier), children now rapidly develop computer skills, soon surpassing their elders; computers are their toys and their learning tools. Fifty years hence we may well conclude that there was no "crisis of American education" in the closing years of the twentieth century—there was only a growing incongruence between the way twentieth-century schools taught and the way late-twentieth-century children learned. Something similar happened in the sixteenth-century university, a hundred years after the invention of the printing press and movable type.

But as to the way we work, the Information Revolution has so far simply routinized what was done all along. The only exception is the CD-ROM, invented around twenty years ago to present operas, university courses, a writer's oeuvre, in an entirely new way. Like the steamboat, the CD-ROM has not immediately caught on.

The Meaning of E-Commerce

E-commerce is to the Information Revolution what the railroad was to the Industrial Revolution—a totally new, totally unprecedented, totally unexpected development. And like the railroad 170 years ago, e-commerce is creating a new and distinct boom, rapidly changing the economy, society, and politics.

One example: A midsize company in America's industrial Midwest, founded in the 1920s and now run by the grandchildren of the founder, used to have some 60 percent of the market in inexpensive dinnerware for fast-food eateries, school and office cafeterias, and hospitals within a hundred-mile radius of its factory. China is heavy and breaks easily, so cheap china is traditionally sold within a small area. Almost overnight this company lost more than half of its market. One of its customers, a hospital cafeteria where someone went "surfing" on the Internet, discovered a European manufacturer that offered china of apparently better quality at a lower price and shipped cheaply by air. Within a few months the main customers in the area shifted to the European supplier. Few of them, it seems, realize—let alone care—that the stuff comes from Europe.

In the new mental geography created by the railroad, humanity mastered distance. In the mental geography of e-commerce, distance has been eliminated. There is only one economy and only one market.

One consequence of this is that every business must become globally competitive, even if it manufactures or sells only within a local or regional market. The competition is not local anymore—in fact, it knows no boundaries. Every company has to become transnational in the way it is run. Yet the traditional multinational may well become obsolete. It manufactures and distributes in a number of distinct geographies, in which it is a *local* company. But in e-commerce there are neither local companies nor distinct geographies. Where to manufacture, where to sell, and how to sell will remain important business decisions. But in another twenty years they may no longer determine what a company does, how it does it, and where it does it.

At the same time, it is not yet clear what kinds of goods and services will be bought and sold through e-commerce and what kinds will turn out to be unsuitable for it. This has been true whenever a new distribution channel has arisen. Why, for instance, did the railroad change both the mental and the economic geography of the West, whereas the steamboat—with its equal impact on world trade and passenger traffic—did neither? Why was there no "steamboat boom"?

Equally unclear has been the impact of more recent changes in distribution channels—in the shift, for instance, from the local grocery store to the supermarket, from the individual supermarket to the supermarket chain, and from the supermarket chain to Wal-Mart and other discount chains. It is already clear that the shift to e-commerce will be just as eclectic and unexpected.

Here are a few examples. Twenty-five years ago it was generally believed that within a few decades the printed word would be dispatched electronically to individual subscribers' computer screens. Subscribers would then either read text on their computer screen or download it and print it out. This was the assumption that underlay the CD-ROM. Thus any number of newspapers and magazines, by no means only in the United States, established themselves on-line; few, so far, have become gold mines. But anyone who twenty years ago predicted the business of Amazon.com and barnesandnoble.com—that is, that books would be sold on the Internet but delivered in their heavy, printed form—would have been laughed off the podium. Yet Amazon.com and barnesandnoble.com are in exactly that business, and they are in it worldwide. The first order for the U.S. edition of my most recent book, *Management Challenges for the 21st Century* (1999), came to Amazon.com, and it came from Argentina.

Another example: Ten years ago one of the world's leading automobile companies made a thorough study of the expected impact on automobile sales of the then emerging Internet. It concluded that the Internet would become a major distribution channel for used cars, but that customers would still want to see new cars, to touch them, to test-drive them. In actuality, at least so far, most used cars are still being bought not over the Internet but in a dealer's lot. However, as many as half of all new cars sold (excluding luxury cars) may now actually be "bought" over the Internet. Dealers only deliver cars that customers have chosen well before they enter the dealership. What does this mean for the future of the local automobile dealership, the twentieth century's most profitable small business?

Another example: *Traders* in the American stock-market boom of 1998 and 1999 increasingly buy and sell on-line. But *investors* seem to be shifting away from buying electronically. The major U.S. investment vehicle is mutual funds. And whereas almost half of all mutual funds a few years ago were bought electronically, it is estimated that the figure will drop to 35 percent next year and to 20 percent by 2005. This is the opposite of what "everybody expected" ten or fifteen years ago.

The fastest-growing e-commerce in the United States is in an area where there was no "commerce" until now— in jobs for professionals and managers. Almost half of the world's largest companies now recruit through Web sites, and some 2.5 million managerial and professional people (two-thirds of them not even engineers or computer professionals) have their résumés on the Internet and solicit job offers over it. The result is a completely new labor market.

This illustrates another important effect of e-commerce. New distribution channels change who the customers are. They change not only *how* customers buy but also *what* they buy. They change consumer behavior, savings patterns, industry structure—in short, the entire economy. This is what is now happening, and not only in the United States but increasingly in the rest of the developed world, and in a good many emerging countries, including mainland China.

Luther, Machiavelli, and the Salmon

The railroad made the Industrial Revolution accomplished fact. What had been revolution became establishment. And the boom it triggered lasted almost a hundred years. The technology of the steam engine did not end with the railroad. It led in the 1880s and 1890s to the steam turbine, and in the 1920s and 1930s to the last magnificent American steam locomotives, so beloved by railroad buffs. But the technology centered on the steam engine and in manufacturing operations ceased to be central. Instead the dynamics of the technology shifted to totally new industries that emerged almost immediately after the railroad was invented, not one of which had anything to do with steam or steam engines. The electric telegraph and photography were first, in the 1830s, followed soon thereafter by optics and farm equipment. The new and different fertilizer industry, which began in the late 1830s, in short order transformed agriculture. Public health became a major and central growth industry, with quarantine, vaccination, the supply of pure water, and sewers, which for the first time in history made the city a more healthful habitat than the countryside. At the same time came the first anesthetics.

With these major new technologies came major new social institutions: the modern postal service, the daily paper, investment banking, and commercial banking, to name just a few. Not one of them had much to do with the steam engine or with the technology of the Industrial Revolution in general. It was these new industries and institutions that by 1850 had come to dominate the industrial and economic landscape of the developed countries.

This is very similar to what happened in the printing revolution—the first of the technological revolutions that created the modern world. In the fifty years after 1455, when Gutenberg had perfected the printing press and movable type he had been working on for years, the printing revolution swept Europe and completely changed its economy and its psychology. But the books printed during the first fifty years, the ones called incunabula, contained largely the same texts that monks, in their scriptoria, had for centuries laboriously copied by hand: religious tracts and whatever remained of the writings of antiquity. Some seven thousand titles were published in those first fifty years, in thirty-five thousand editions. At least sixty-seven hundred of these were traditional titles. In other words, in its first fifty years, printing made available—and increasingly cheap—traditional information and communication products. But then, some sixty years after Gutenberg, came Luther's German Bible—thousands and thousands of copies sold almost immediately at an unbelievably low price. With Luther's Bible the new printing technology ushered in a new society. It ushered in Protestantism, which conquered half of Europe and, within another twenty years, forced the Catholic Church to reform itself in the other half. Luther used the new medium of print deliberately to restore religion to the center of individual life and of society. And this unleashed a century and a half of religious reform, religious revolt, religious wars.

At the very same time, however, that Luther used print with the avowed intention of restoring Christianity, Machiavelli wrote and published *The Prince* (1513), the first Western book in more than a thousand years that contained not one biblical quotation and no reference to the writers of antiquity. In no time at all *The Prince* became the "other best-seller" of the sixteenth century, and its most notorious but also most influential book. In short order there was a wealth of purely secular works, what we today call literature: novels and books in science, history, politics, and soon, economics. It was not long before the first purely secular art form arose, in England—the modern theater. Brand-new social institutions also arose: the Jesuit order, the Spanish infantry, the first modern navy, and finally, the sovereign national state. In other words, the printing revolution followed the same trajectory as did the Industrial Revolution, which began three hundred years later, and as does the Information Revolution today.

What the new industries and institutions will be, no one can say yet. No one in the 1520s anticipated secular literature, let alone the secular theater. No one in the 1820s anticipated the electric telegraph, or public health, or photography.

The one thing (to say it again) that is highly probable, if not nearly certain, is that the next twenty years will see the emergence of a number of new industries. At the same time, it is nearly certain that few of them will come out of information technology, the computer, data processing, or the Internet. This is indicated by all historical precedents. But it is true also of the new industries that are already rapidly emerging. Biotechnology, as mentioned, is already here. So is fish farming.

Twenty-five years ago salmon was a delicacy. The typical convention dinner gave a choice between chicken and beef. Today salmon is a commodity and is the other choice on the convention menu. Most salmon today is not caught at sea or in a river but grown on a fish farm. The same is increasingly true of trout. Soon, apparently, it will be true of a number of other fish. Flounder, for instance, which is to seafood what pork is to meat, is just going into oceanic mass production. This will no doubt lead to the genetic development of new and different fish, just as the domestication of sheep, cows, and chickens led to the development of new breeds among them.

But probably a dozen or so technologies are at the stage where biotechnology was twenty-five years ago—that is, ready to emerge.

There is also a *service* waiting to be born: insurance against the risks of foreign-exchange exposure. Now that every business is part of the global economy, such insurance is as badly needed as was insurance against physical risks (fire, flood) in the early stages of the Industrial Revolution, when traditional insurance emerged. All the knowledge needed for foreign-exchange insurance is available; only the institution itself is still lacking.

The next two or three decades are likely to see even greater technological change than has occurred in the decades since the emergence of the computer, and also even greater change in industry structures, in the economic landscape, and probably in the social landscape as well.

The Gentleman versus the Technologist

The new industries that emerged after the railroad owed little technologically to the steam engine or to the Industrial Revolution in general. They were not its "children after the flesh"—but they were its "children after the spirit." They were possible only because of the mind-set that the Industrial Revolution had created and the skills it had developed. This was a mind-set that accepted— indeed, eagerly welcomed—invention and innovation. It was a mind-set that accepted, and eagerly welcomed, new products and new services.

It also created the social values that made possible the new industries. Above all, it created the "technologist."

Social and financial success long eluded the first major American technologist, Eli Whitney, whose cotton gin, in 1793, was as central to the triumph of the Industrial Revolution as was the steam engine. But a generation later the technologist—still self-taught—had become the American folk hero and was both socially accepted and financially rewarded. Samuel Morse, the inventor of the telegraph, may have been the first example: Thomas Edison became the most prominent. In Europe the "businessman" long remained a social inferior, but the university-trained engineer had by 1830 or 1840 become a respected "professional."

By the 1850s England was losing its predominance and beginning to be overtaken as an industrial economy, first by the United States and then by Germany. It is generally accepted that neither economics nor technology was the major reason. The main cause was social. Economically, and especially financially, England remained the great power until the First World War. Technologically it held its own throughout the nineteenth century. Synthetic dyestuffs, the first products of the modern chemical industry, were invented in England, and so was the steam turbine. But England did not accept the technologist socially. He never became a "gentleman." The English built first-rate engineering schools in India but almost none at home. No other country so honored the "scientist"—and, indeed, Britain retained leadership in physics throughout the nineteenth century, from James Clerk Maxwell and Michael Faraday all the way to Ernest Rutherford. But the technologist remained a "tradesman." (Dickens, for instance, showed open contempt for the upstart ironmaster in his 1853 novel, *Bleak House*.)

Nor did England develop the venture capitalist, who has the means and the mentality to finance the unexpected and unproved. A French invention, first portrayed in Balzac's monumental *La Comédie humaine,* in the 1840s, the venture capitalist was institutionalized in the United States by J. P. Morgan and, simultaneously, in Germany and Japan by the universal bank. But England, although it invented and developed the commercial bank to finance trade, had no institution to finance industry until two German refugees, S. G. Warburg and Henry Grunfeld, started an entrepreneurial bank in London, just before the Second World War.

Bribing the Knowledge Worker

What might be needed to prevent the United States from becoming the England of the twenty-first century? I am convinced that a drastic change in the social mind-set is required—just as leadership in the industrial economy after the railroad required the drastic change from "tradesman" to "technologist" or "engineer."

What we call the Information Revolution is actually a Knowledge Revolution. What has made it possible to routinize processes is not machinery; the computer is only the trigger. Software is the reorganization of traditional work, based on centuries of experience, through the application of knowledge and especially of systematic, logical analysis. The key is not electronics; it is cognitive science. This means that the key to maintaining leadership in the economy and the technology that are about to emerge is likely to be the social position of knowledge professionals and social acceptance of their values. For them to remain traditional "employees" and be treated as such would be tantamount to England's treating its technologists as tradesmen—and likely to have similar consequences.

Today, however, we are trying to straddle the fence—to maintain the traditional mind-set, in which capital is the key resource and the financier is the boss, while bribing knowledge workers to be content to remain employees by giving them bonuses and stock options. But this, if it can work at all, can work only as long as the emerging industries enjoy a stock-market boom, as the Internet companies have been doing. The next major industries are likely to behave far more like traditional industries—that is, to grow slowly, painfully, laboriously.

The early industries of the Industrial Revolution—cotton textiles, iron, the railroads—were boom industries that created millionaires overnight, like Balzac's venture bankers and like Dickens's ironmaster, who in a few years grew from a lowly domestic servant into a "captain of industry." The industries that emerged after 1830 also created millionaires. But they took twenty years to do so, and it was twenty years of hard work, of struggle, of disappointments and failures, of thrift. This is likely to be true of the industries that will emerge from now on. It is already true of biotechnology.

Bribing the knowledge workers on whom these industries depend will therefore simply not work. The key knowledge workers in these businesses will surely continue to expect to share financially in the fruits of their labor. But the financial fruits are likely to take much longer to ripen, if they ripen at all. And then, probably within ten years or so, running a business with (short-term) "shareholder value" as its first—if not its only—goal and justification will have become counterproductive. Increasingly, performance in these new knowledge-based industries will come to depend on running the institution so as to attract, hold, and motivate knowledge workers. When this can no longer be done by satisfying knowledge workers' greed, as we are now trying to do, it will have to be done by satisfying their values, and by giving them social recognition and social power. It will have to be done by turning them from subordinates into fellow executives, and from employees, however well paid, into partners.

(1999)

2

The Exploding World of the Internet

This interview was conducted by Mark Williams, contributing editor of *Red Herring* magazine, in the author's office in Claremont, California. It was based on the author's specifying the topics and the interviewer's questions. The author himself edited the interviewer's draft into the final text. The interview appeared in the January 30, 2001, issue of *Red Herring*.

You've said that giving knowledge workers stock options amounts to nothing more than bribing them with a currency that will have diminished value after the stock market boom subsides. It won't work, you've claimed.

I told some of my friends and clients five years ago that we've plenty of experience with this, especially if you've been around as long as I have. Financial incentives don't prevent people from leaving. They motivate people to leave, because the moment they can get that bonus or exercise those options, then the immediate financial gain becomes their only motivation.

Companies that have gone in most for these things have had the greatest turnover. IBM once had the largest alumni association in the world. No longer. It's incredible the number of ex-Microsoft people I've encountered. Furthermore, those two alumni associations which were the largest—Procter & Gamble and IBM—those alumni love their ex-companies. Microsoft alumni hate Microsoft. Precisely because they feel the one thing it offered them was money and nothing else, they resent that all the publicity goes to the top people, to one top man, and they don't get recognition. Also, they feel the value system is entirely financial, and they see themselves as professionals. Maybe not scientists, but applied scientists. So their value system is different.

Recently, I spoke with a high-tech company I've seen grow over fifty years from babyhood into a big company—we're talking about $10 billion in sales. I was there for one day, but for two weeks this meeting of senior management was focused on holding knowledge people. Their turnover rate—they're not in Silicon Valley—had become frightening. Before this meeting, they did something I'd suggested. They went to senior researchers and technical staff who'd left and asked why. The answer they received was "Whenever I came to talk to one of you, all you talked about was the stock price." One fellow said,

"I spent six weeks in China with our three main customers there, and when I returned and went to the head of international technical service, I sat for an hour trying to talk about the opportunities I see in China. All that interested him was that our stock went down eight points the day before."

That isn't fun. Management increasingly will have to balance their knowledge of people's values against the concern with immediate financial results, which won't subside while the stock market does well. If I sound like an old financial man now, I am, you know. But we believed that when you see that the trading volume isn't people who buy shares or who sell shares, but traders buying and selling short term, then the market has gotten out of control.

I understand you were an investment banker in London.

I left the financial business sixty-three years ago and haven't been interested in it since. Still, anybody who knows anything knew six months ago that Intel would have a bad period. It's a period of change in which one must invest in things that, firstly, have high risk and, secondly, require some years. Anybody who understands anything understood that. Yet when they published it, Intel's stock just disappeared. That's an unstable market.

So companies can no longer drive knowledge workers with stock options?

You've heard the human resources adage that you cannot hire a hand, the whole man always comes with it? Well, you cannot just hire a man, the spouse always comes with it. And the spouse has already spent that stock option money. I'm not joking. Nothing is more dangerous than profit sharing, stock options, and such that don't meet expectations.

Haven't you said that important knowledge workers will have to be made full partners, rather than mere shareholders?

Yes. I am talking of things that I'm working on. These aren't matters I'm positive about yet. In many cases, it will make more sense to work with highly specialized senior people as independent contractors.

We need to measure knowledge workers' productivity. How do we do that?

We begin by asking even lower-level knowledge workers three things: What are your strengths and what should you put work into? What should this company expect from you and in what time span? And what information do you need to do your work and what information do you owe?

I learned this many years ago when I worked with one of the world's biggest pharmaceutical companies. A new CEO expected each department head to explain what their function should contribute. The head of research said, "You can't measure research." So we arranged meetings with eleven to thirteen people at a time, working through the research department. I asked, "Looking over the last five years, what have you contributed which made a difference? What do you think you can contribute in the next three years?" Suppose they'd found some hormonal function that changed our understanding of how the pancreas works. It might be twenty years, if ever, before that became a product. However, repeatedly—this was the early 1960s—there'd been important contributions that evaporated. They didn't fit the market for pharmaceutical companies or how the medical director saw the company. So we had to change that. We brought the medical, marketing, and manufacturing people into what was happening in research. They doubled the utilization—the yield from research—within five or six years.

What about American health care, which seems mired in contradictions?

It's no worse than any other country's. They're all bankrupt. It'll be a growth sector simply because health care and education together will be 40 percent of the gross national product within twenty years. Already, they're at least a third.

Furthermore, as more and more services by government agencies will be outsourced, it will make little difference whether the organization which gets a contract to clean the streets is for profit or not for profit. It won't be in the market economy. If I could voice one comment on your magazine and the present e-commerce and e-business-to-business concern altogether, it's so far focused on business. Yet I think the greatest e-commerce impact may be in higher education and health care. It makes possible a rational restructuring of health care. Eighty percent of demands in health care require only a nurse-practitioner. What she needs to know is when to refer a patient to a physician, which largely now can become a matter of using information technology.

I've worked with hospitals which are the only ones within two hundred miles. It's incredible what a difference information technology has made to them. Take Grand Junction, Colorado, with thirty-four thousand inhabitants. Denver and Salt Lake City—two sizable cities—are both about two hundred miles away. Now Grand Junction's hospital can make a diagnosis of a patient which brings in the University of Colorado medical school in Denver and whatever medical school Salt Lake City has. That answers that small hospital's basic problem, which was that they couldn't build their own specialist center.

Was this that hospital's only problem? Could it even be profitable, given that area's population base?

You may have a million people for whom Grand Junction represents the nearest decent hospital. I've worked with a consortium of twenty-five such hospitals, from West Virginia to Oregon. Information technology can make them the equivalent of a big-city university hospital. With that patient with convulsions and vertigo that nobody in Grand Junction can diagnose, for example, now the doctor says, this may be a thyroid problem and we'll talk to Salt Lake City. The specialist in Salt Lake City diagnoses a cyst on the thyroid pressing the carotid—this was an actual case—and says, "I've done some of those, but my colleague in Denver is better. Helicopter him there." Three days later, the patient is back in Grand Junction.

Thus, in health care, information technology has already made a fabulous impact. In education, its impact will be greater. However, attempts to put ordinary college courses on the Internet are a mistake. Marshall McLuhan was correct. The medium not only controls how things are communicated, but what things are communicated. On the Web, you must do it differently.

How so?

You must redesign everything. Firstly, you must hold students' attention. Any good teacher has a radar system to get the class's reaction, but you don't have that on-line. Secondly, you must enable students to do what they cannot do in a college course, which is go back and forth. So on-line you must combine a book's qualities with a course's continuity and flow. Above all, you must put it in a context. In a college course, the college provides the context. In that on-line course you turn on at home, the course must provide the background, the context, the references.

What about on-line education's potential in the developing world? For example, the Indian government has begun a program to put an on-line PC in each village for education.

My prejudices show. In the early 1950s, President Truman sent me to Brazil to persuade the government there that with the new technology, we could wipe out illiteracy in five years at no cost. The Brazilian teachers' union sabotaged it. We have possessed the technology to eliminate illiteracy for a long time.

Let me point out that the one great achievement of

Mao's government was to eliminate illiteracy in China. Not by means of a new technology, but a very old one: the student who has learned to read teaches the next one. Teachers have obstructed this everywhere because it threatens their monopoly. Yet older students teaching younger students is the quickest way. It's what the Chinese have done. For the first time the great majority of Chinese understand and can speak Mandarin. You have the country unified not only by script, but by language. It's still only 70 percent. But it was 30 when Mao came in.

We can make the new technology available to the remotest village in the Amazon. The obstacles are, first, enormous resistance by teachers, who see themselves threatened. Secondly, it isn't true that you've support for education in every third-world country. I worked hard in Colombia and helped found the Universidad del Valle in Cali. We had a very difficult time in those small coffee-growing towns because parents expected children to be at work in the fields at age eleven.

In India that's a great problem. Moreover, schools are an equalizing force. That's a tremendous obstacle in Indian provinces like Orissa, say, where the upper castes would bitterly fight admission of lower-class children.

Let's return to health care. Some people insist that market forces can be a cure-all for U.S. health care. Given situations like these rural hospitals where little opportunity for profit exists, is that true?

No. Market forces cannot be the cure-all for health care. I always put my cards on the table. I have been the consultant to two major national health care systems. One for fifty years, one for thirty. The idea that American health care is in particularly bad shape is nonsense. They're all in total disarray. The reason is that they're based on the facts of 1900. The worst is either the German or the Japanese. As I said, 80 percent of demands on a health care system are routine problems a nurse-practitioner can handle. You face two issues with a nurse-practitioner. First, you must ensure she doesn't go beyond her competence, so you emphasize she should overrefer to the medical center, not underrefer. The second problem is that a nurse-practitioner doesn't have the authority to change anybody's lifestyle. For three thousand years we've built the mystique of the M.D. When the doctor says you must lose fifteen pounds, and the nurse-practitioner says it, you hear something different.

Then there's the 20 percent of health care which requires modern medicine. Incidentally, I'm going to shock you. Medical advances since antibiotics have had no impact on life expectancy. They are wonderful for tiny groups, but statistically insignificant. The great changes have been in the workforce. When I was born, 95 percent of all people worked in manual jobs—most of them dangerous, debilitating jobs. You've heard of Franz Kafka, haven't you?

Of course.

You know he was a great writer, don't you? But Franz Kafka also invented the safety helmet. He was the great man in factory inspection and workmen's compensation.

Kafka was the workmen's compensation–factory safety man for what's now the Czech Republic, which was Bohemia and Moravia before World War I. Our next-door neighbor was the top workmen's compensation–factory safety man for Austria. Kafka was his idol. When Kafka [was dying] outside of Vienna of throat tuberculosis, Dr. Kuiper—our neighbor—pedaled on his bike at five each morning for two hours to visit the dying Kafka, then took the train to work. After Kafka's death, nobody was more surprised than Dr. Kuiper to discover he'd been a writer. Kafka got the gold medal of, I think, the American Safety Congress for 1912 because as a result of his safety helmet, the steel mills in what is [now] the Czech Republic for the first time killed fewer than twenty-five workers per one thousand a year.

Did you know that Blue Cross and Blue Shield of Massachusetts employs as many people to administer coverage for 2.5 million New Englanders as are employed in Canada to administer coverage for 27 million Canadians?

Yes. And it isn't true. You are comparing . . .

Apples and oranges?

No. Apples and beavers. The Canadian system doesn't administer health care. It pays fixed rates, that's all. What we do now, the Canadian system doesn't. It doesn't tell any doctor what to do. It just says, for this you get X dollars in Ontario and Y dollars in Saskatchewan. Blue Cross—in Massachusetts particularly—is trying to be an HMO: a health care provider, not a health care payer. The Canadian system is not managed care, it's managed costs.

What should happen with American health care?

Let me say that if we had listened to Mr. Eisenhower, who wanted catastrophic health care for everybody, we would have no health care problems. What shut him down, as you may not have heard, was the UAW. In the 1950s, the only benefit the unions could still promise was company-paid health care. Under the Eisenhower principle—where for everybody who spent more than 10 percent of their taxable income for health expenditures, government would pay—this would have been eliminated. So the UAW killed it with help from the American Medical Association. Still, the AMA wasn't that powerful. The UAW was.

You've talked about demographic changes, with more old people in the developed nations and more younger people, for the next forty years, in the developing nations. Do you worry how it will be for the young in a world dominated by the old?

Look. In the developed countries, with the exception of the U.S., the number of young people is already going down sharply. In the U.S., it will begin diminishing in fifteen or eighteen years. Since 1700, we've tacitly assumed that population grows, and the foundation grows faster than the top. So this is unprecedented. We have no idea what it means.

There are indications. We know that in the Chinese coastal cities, the middle class spends more on the one child they are allowed than they used to spend on all four that they had before. Those kids are horribly spoiled.

That's true in this country, too. When I look at what ten-year-olds expect to own, it's unthinkable for my generation.

Also, when you say young people, in the developed countries that will mean, very heavily, immigrants, not children. They're immigrants, whether a Mexican entering southern California, a Nigerian entering Spain, or a Ukrainian entering Germany. These will be young, in that the average age of an immigrant into the developed countries is between eighteen and twenty-eight. They represent a very heavy capital investment in their upbringing, yet aren't adequately educated. We don't know what that means. Perhaps tremendous additional productive power and tremendous demand for additional educational expenses. We don't know, we've never been there.

But it is predictable that today's youth culture will not last forever. It's an old insight that the prevailing culture is made by the fastest-growing population group. That will not be young people.

Today we can buy for $10 a wristwatch more reliable and durable than the clockwork items companies once doled out to retiring employees. In the automobile industry, which increasingly refines its designs so cars become safer and more dependable, the same trend is visible. As this trend dominates more and more industries, how will corporations compete?

I, with my clients, go on a simple assumption: You cannot survive as a manufacturing company. You must become a knowledge company based on distribution. You cannot really differentiate products in manufacturing.

The automobile industry is interesting. A car's relative price against the price of thirty years ago is 40 percent less. Conversely, many automobile customers have shifted to the sports utility vehicle. Probably, adjusted for inflation and the relative purchasing power of knowledge, what those people pay isn't much less than they paid thirty years ago. Manufactured goods' prices, adjusted for inflation, are down 40 percent since the Kennedy years, and the cost of the two main knowledge products, education and health care, is three times inflation. In fact, the relative purchasing power of manufactured goods is maybe one-quarter of what it was forty years ago. Yet the automobile industry—and it's the only one—has been compensated by people buying these more expensive vehicles. Still, though a large proportion of the population buys these vehicles, they drive [them] so much longer. Those vehicles are only short-term profit centers.

Long term? Forty percent of the automobile-buying public in America once bought a new car every two years. Now, in the parking lot for our college's advanced executive program, I don't think there's a single car younger than five years. So, an automobile company can survive as a manufacturing company, though there's no product differentiation. Yes, one point of market share is worth God knows how much. However, you take it from someone else. As far as the industry is concerned, nobody makes more money.

Therefore, you must become a distribution company

based on knowledge about the database. This is the great shift. It's comparable to what happened since World War I in agriculture. The output in volume of products is rising very fast. In terms of percentage of national product, it's diminishing very fast. In terms of employment, it's shrinking very fast. Manufacturing does not add value anymore. Value is contributed in knowledge and distributing.

Coming to America during the Great Depression, when intellectuals had mostly signed on with collective ideologies, you were independent enough to realize that corporations could be "the place in which and through which the social tasks would be organized." But today we see events—like the demonstrations in Seattle—showing that the Marxist critique of Victorian-era capitalism still overshadows how many people see corporations. What might change that?

Let me say that there are very serious reasons why those assorted demonstrators are a motley crowd, have nothing in common, and will not make much impact. We are not going into worldwide free trade. The decline in manufacturing will force us into protectionism. Look, for every shrinkage of 1 percent in agriculture and farm employment, farm subsidies in all developed countries have risen 2 percent since World War II. Expect the same in manufacturing. We aren't going into a free market in goods and services. Free market means free market in information. In goods and services—goods, especially— there will be increasing protectionism. The fewer jobs, the more protection. We've been through that in farming. You will see it in manufacturing.

The new Mexican president, Mr. Fox, is right that the more rapidly we integrate Mexico into the North American economy, the better. You can't possibly expect development on yesterday's basis of export-led development. While the Mexican birthrate is dropping faster than anywhere else in the world—from four or five children for each woman of reproductive age, it's down to below two, and it'll probably be below one in ten years—an enormous number of people are reaching age twenty from the high-birthrate years of twenty years ago, when infant mortality dropped sharply. The only choice is, will these people be low-paid workers in southern California or even lower-paid ones in Mexico? I don't think we have a choice.

Mr. Fox is absolutely right, because he sees the North American region as a protected, highly subsidized area, like the European Economic Community is in agriculture and is becoming in manufacturing. Incidentally, the ones most threatened by this development are the Japanese, because there is no East Asian economic area—and if one emerges, China will dominate it.

So, the protesters against globalization not only have a point—sure, they protest against the wrong things— but they feel the pain. U.S. policy of the last thirty years, pushing for free trade anyplace, assumes the U.S. has the advantage in most areas. Which we had because of our knowledge base. I don't think you can take that for granted. I wouldn't say we're endangered, but there's every reason to believe that other areas will catch up.

I think you will see regional protectionism. You will also see growing environmental pressure against globalization. Have you ever been to Indonesia? All the controls are on the statute books, but the pollution is unbelievable. Bali is being destroyed by pollution. Export of pollution will bring growing pressure to control it.

And immigration is becoming the central political issue everyplace. From that point of view, these protesters are not post-Marxists—though there are ex-Marxists among them.

These aren't just children of affluence looking for a focus?

So far, these protests have no focus. They are protests against the system, whatever that means.

We have shifted very heavily from being labor-intensive to capital-intensive. So far that has compensated for the loss of relative purchasing power of manufacturing goods. How much longer will that continue? I don't know.

But all the world over, the blue-collar manufacturing worker is losing something more important than income. He's losing status. So he's protesting against globalization, which he thinks means the exporting of jobs. Hell, no! The number of jobs being exported is minimal. It's so small it ain't funny! It's the jobs at home that are being changed totally.

We will see more of these protests. They are hitting out against yesterday's targets, but they are hitting out because of today's pain.

(2001)

3

From Computer Literacy to Information Literacy

The first management conference we know of was called in 1882 by the German Post Office. The topic—and only chief executive officers were invited—was how not to be afraid of the telephone. Nobody showed up. The invitees were insulted. The idea that they should use telephones was unthinkable. The telephone was for underlings.

I was reminded of this story in the early 1960s when I was working with IBM to make computers accessible to executives. Back then, some of us already understood this wasn't just another gimmick—that it was something that would profoundly, even fundamentally, change the way we organize industry and do business. Information would become the main productivity factor.

IBM's Tom Watson Jr. came up with a brilliant idea.

43

We would have a meeting for CEOs and talk about "computer literacy." In fact, it was on that occasion that we coined the term.

However, I immediately tried to talk Watson out of this brilliant idea. I told him the story of the German Post Office. "You're at that same stage," I said. "Nobody's going to show up. It's too weird for them."

Twenty-five or thirty years ago that kind of meeting was indeed not possible. Thirty years from now such meetings will not be necessary because today's CEOs will have been succeeded by their grandchildren's generation.

Anyone who knows this generation, who has children between the ages of ten and thirteen, won't be surprised by what I learned while visiting my youngest daughter and her children. My grandson, a very nice boy, is at thirteen no longer into computers. Kid stuff, he says, except for parallel processing. However, he keeps his hand in, you might say. He said to me, "Grandfather, Daddy's computer is no longer state-of-the-art."

The joke? My son-in-law happens to be a physics professor who runs one of the bigger nonmilitary computer installations in existence. But my grandson was right.

When this generation grows up and moves into our jobs, we won't have to talk about computer literacy. Just as we no longer have to talk about how not to be afraid of the telephone. My grandson's five-year-old sister can dial the world over. And does.

Of course, my grandson is not the only one who is

computer literate. In this country, his whole generation is. This is one area where we are way ahead. Computer literacy is in its infancy in Japan and is still unheard of in Europe. My wife has nieces and nephews in Germany, and their children know nothing, though as it happens the parents are both scientists. The parents work with computers, but the idea that a nine- or ten-year-old should be familiar with computers is a new one.

Even though we are way ahead on this one, we're still not quite where we should be. We must be computer literate in self-defense. Ten or fifteen years hence, not only will we take computer literacy for granted, we will have become information literate as well.

And that, very few people are.

Most CEOs still believe that it's the chief information officer's job to identify the information the CEO requires. This is, of course, a fallacy. The information officer is a toolmaker; the CEO is the tool user.

Let me illustrate. Recently, I got around to repairing the overstuffed sofa in our guest room, which I should have repaired three years ago. At the hardware store, I asked the owner which upholstery hammer would be best for the task. I didn't ask him whether I should repair the sofa. That decision was my job. I merely asked him for the right tool. And he gave it to me.

When I had my fax machine installed a few years ago, I had the telephone installer come in to put in a new line, and he was very helpful. He looked around and said to me, "You may have chosen the wrong place to put it. I think it would be awkward over there. Why not here? And I can easily give you a line here, too." But he didn't tell me to whom to send faxes or what to say in them. This is my job. His job was to give me the tool.

CEOs must accept that if the computer is a tool, it is the tool user's job to decide how to use it. They must learn to assume "information responsibility." Which means asking, What information do I need to do my job? From whom? In what form? When? As well as, What information do I owe? To whom? In what form? When? Unfortunately, most people still expect the chief information officer or some other technologist to answer those questions. This won't do.

I teach at a small graduate school, Claremont. About twelve years ago, we wanted to have a computer sciences building built. When it came to raising the money, we beat out Stanford and Yale. We got an enormous amount of corporate money because we said in our proposal, "This school will not be in business in ten years. If we do a halfway decent job, it will have become superfluous. In ten years there will be computer engineers, there will be people who design software. But computer science as a separate discipline in a management school will be gone."

We got all of this money simply because we said that in ten or fifteen years we will not have to spend a lot of time creating toolmakers. We'll need them, of course. But users will know how to use the tools; toolmaking will remain important but purely technical.

The first step is to take information responsibility: What information do I need to do my job? In what form? The information specialists can then say, Look, you can't get it in this form; you can get it in that form. The answer is relatively unimportant and technical; it is the basic questions that count: When do I need it? From whom? What information do I owe?

We are rebuilding organizations around information. When CEOs talk of eliminating management levels, they begin to use information as a structural element. Many times, we quickly discover that most management levels manage nothing. Instead, they merely amplify the faint signals emanating from the top and bottom of the corporate infrastructure. I imagine that most CEOs have heard the first law of information theory: Every relay doubles the noise and cuts the message in half. The same holds true for most management levels, which neither manage people nor make decisions. They serve only as relays. When we build in information as a structural element, we don't need such levels.

This, however, creates enormous problems. For instance, where will we look for opportunities for promotion? Few businesses will have more than two or three layers. Will CEOs be able to accept that more layers are a sign of poor organization? You violate a basic rule. Very few people get into a management job before they are twenty-six or twenty-seven. You have to be in a job five years not only to learn it, but to prove yourself. And yet you have to be young enough to be considered for senior management jobs before you reach fifty. That gives you three levels of management.

If you look at the General Motors of today versus that of yesterday, you'll see it's slimmed down a bit. The company used to have twenty-nine layers, which meant that nobody could really be considered for a top management job before age two hundred and eleven. This, obviously, is part of GM's problem.

Where will the promotion opportunities come from? How will we reward and recognize people? Also, how will we prepare people for jobs that are not functionally narrow?

These are big challenges. And we don't know the answers. We know only that we will pay much more. Money will become far more important because in the past thirty years, we have substituted title for money in many cases. We have had rapid promotions in title with very little increase in salary. That's over.

Far more important is the change in the process. When we learn to use information as a tool, we are learning what to use it for, what we need, in what form, when, from whom, and so on. The moment you examine these questions, you realize that the information you need—the really important information—you cannot truly get from your information system. Your information system gives you inside information. But there are no results inside a business.

Many, many years ago, I coined the term *profit center*. I am thoroughly ashamed of it now, because inside a business there are no profit centers, just cost centers. Profit comes only from the outside. When a customer returns with a repeat order and his check doesn't bounce, you have a profit center. Until then you have only cost centers.

When we talk about the global economy, I hope nobody believes it can be managed. It can't. There is no information on it. But if you are in the hospital field, you can know hospitals. If you were to parachute into some strange place and make your way to the lights in the valley, you would be able to identify the correct building as the hospital. Even in Inner Mongolia, I can assure you that you will know you are in a hospital. No mistaking it. No mistaking a school. No mistaking a restaurant.

People who tell me they operate in a world economy are those whose shares I sell immediately. One cannot operate where one can't know anything. We simply have no information at all. You can't know everything. You can know only what you know. This is why the enterprise of tomorrow is going to be very narrow in focus.

Diversification can work only if you have the information. And you don't have it if the competition can come in from Osaka without any warning. We have so little information on the outside, on markets, on customers. Nothing—as many people have learned the hard way—is changing faster than distribution channels. And if you wait until you get the report, it's way too late.

Technology itself provides the perfect illustration. It's no longer the nineteenth century, or even the twentieth, when you could assume that technologies pertaining to and affecting your industry came out of your industry.

Time has overthrown the idea behind the great research labs, of which IBM's is probably the last. There will be no other like it. Most of what really had an impact on the computer and the computer industry did not come out of IBM's lab. IBM couldn't use most of the brilliant things that came out of its lab in its own business. And that holds true of Bell Labs and of the pharmaceutical labs.

Technology is no longer a series of parallel streams that in the nineteenth century underlay our academic disciplines. Instead, it is a crisscross. It is chaotic and therefore has to come from outside. And about this outside we know nothing.

Here you are, a pharmaceutical manufacturer. You are going to be made obsolete by mechanical instruments or processes—say, by a pacemaker or a bypass. You may have the world's best lab, but the changes in your business will not come out of your lab. Your lab is focused on the inside, as is your information system.

In effect, we are trying to fly on one wing, the wing of inside information. The big challenge will not be to get more or better inside information, but to add outside information.

To cite an example: Most people believe this country has a balance-of-trade deficit. Most people are wrong but don't know it. The early-eighteenth-century balance-of-trade concept was developed when a bright cookie had an idea. But this brilliant idea was limited to merchandise trade, and that is the only figure reported.

Although this country today has a merchandise trade deficit, it also happens to have an enormous service trade surplus. The official amount is two-thirds of the merchandise trade deficit. The actual figure is probably much bigger, because the real service trade figures are simply not there.

For instance, we have some five hundred thousand foreign students in this country; the minimum they bring in is $15,000 each. Therefore, we have about $7 to $8 billion in foreign-exchange income from these non-American students. It is simply not reported. I believe we may actually have a total merchandise and service surplus, though only a very small one. The figures aren't there, only the concept.

Our biggest challenge will continue to be obtaining this outside information so that we can make good decisions. This relates to the domestic market, the way customers are changing and the way distribution systems are changing. It also relates to technology and competition, because both can put you out of business. When the pacemaker hit, the market for the most profitable cardiac medicine disappeared in five years. It was only after the market had disappeared that people stopped to ask what had happened.

We need outside information, and we will have to learn. But it is complicated because most businesses have two information systems. One is organized around the data stream; the other, far older one, around the accounting system. The accounting system, though, is a five-hundred-year-old information system that is in terrible shape. The changes we will see in information technologies over the next twenty years are nothing compared to the changes we will see in accounting.

We have already begun to observe changes in manufacturing cost accounting, whose roots go back to the 1920s and which is totally obsolete. But that is only for manufacturing, not service. Manufacturing today accounts for 23 percent of the GNP and perhaps 16 percent of employment. Thus, for the vast majority of businesses we have no accounting that's worth anything.

The problem with service-business accounting is simple. Whether it's a department store or a university or a hospital, we know how much money comes in and we know how much money goes out. We even know where it goes. But we cannot relate expenditures to results. Nobody knows how.

At present, these two systems are separate. They will not be separate for our grandchildren's generation. Today's CEOs still depend on the accounting model. I don't know of a single business that bases its decisions on the data processing stream. Everyone bases their decisions on the accounting model, even though most of us have learned how easy this model is to manipulate.

We know where we can trust it and where we can't. We have all fallen through thin ice often enough not to walk on every part of it. We have learned to depend on cash flow because any second-year accounting student can manipulate a P&L. By the next generation, when the data processing stream is more familiar, we will be able to merge the two, or at least make them compatible, which they aren't today. We teach them separately in the schools.

We have an accounting major and a computer science major, and the two don't talk to each other. Both departments are, as a rule, headed by people who know little about information. The person who heads up your accounting system knows government requirements. The head of data processing came up in hardware. Neither knows information.

We will have to bring the two together, but we don't yet know how. My own guess is that ten years from now a medium-size company, let alone a large one, will have two different people filling two positions that one person handles today. It will have a chief financial officer, who will not manage anybody. This person will manage the corporation's money, the biggest part of which will be managing foreign exchange—tough now and soon to become much worse. And the company will have a chief information officer, who will manage its information systems. The company will need both. They look at the world and the business quite differently.

Neither of these people, though, is focused on the *wealth-producing capacity* of the business or on tomorrow's decisions. They are both focused on what happened. Not on what *might* happen or could be *made* to happen.

We have an enormous job ahead of us. We need to make ourselves and our businesses information literate. That job will begin with the individual. We must become tool users. We need to look on information as a tool for a specific job, which few people do. (Most who approach information in this way are not in business; those who have gone the furthest are in the military.)

Our second big job is to use our data processing capacity to understand what is happening on the outside. The available data are usually in poor form and of dubious reliability. The only companies that have any information of this kind are the big Japanese trading houses. They have information about the outside (what they have about Brazil is amazing), but it took them forty years and a great deal of money to acquire it.

For most CEOs, the most important information is not

about customers but about noncustomers. This is the group in which change will occur.

Let's take a look at that endangered species, the American department store. Nobody knew more about their customers than did these stores. Until the 1980s they held on to their customers. But they had no information about noncustomers. They had 28 percent of the retail market, the largest single share. However, this meant that 72 percent didn't shop at the department stores. And the department stores had no information on these people. And they couldn't have cared less. Thus, they were unaware that new customers—especially the affluent—do not shop in department stores. Nobody knows why. They just don't. By the end of the 1980s, though, these noncustomers had become the dominant influence group. They began to determine how all of us shop. But nobody in the department store world knew this because they had been looking at their own customers. After a time, they knew more and more about less and less.

We must begin to organize information from the outside, where the true profit centers exist. We will have to build a system that gives this information to those who make the decisions. And we will have to bring together the accounting and data processing systems, which is something few people are interested in doing. We're at the beginning.

If you are not computer literate, do not expect anyone in your organization to respect you. The young people in your businesses take it for granted; they expect at least literacy from the boss. My five-year-old granddaughter would have no respect for me if I told her, "You know, I'm afraid of the telephone." She wouldn't even believe me.

Times change, and we must change with them. We are moving from minimal computer literacy—knowing little more than the ABCs and multiplication tables of computing—to the point where we can really do something with computers. That will be an exciting and challenging prospect for the years ahead.

We are just entering that stream. It's going to be a fast one.

(1998)

4

E-Commerce:
The Central Challenge

Traditional multinationals will, in time, be killed by e-commerce. The e-commerce delivery of goods, of services, of repairs, spare parts, and maintenance will require a different organization from that of any multinational today. It will also require a different mind-set, a different top management, and in the end, different definitions of performance. Indeed, the very way performance is measured will change.

In most businesses today delivery is considered a "support" function, a routine to be taken care of by clerks. It is taken for granted unless something goes dramatically wrong. But under e-commerce, delivery will become the one area in which a business can truly distinguish itself. It will become the critical "core competence." Its speed, quality, and responsiveness may well become the decisive competitive factor even where brands seem to be entrenched. And no existing multinational and altogether very few businesses are organized for it. Very few yet even think that way.

The railway, invented in 1829, mastered distance. This explains why, more than any other of the inventions of the Industrial Revolution, the railway changed every nation's economy and workforce. It changed humanity's mind-set, its horizon, its "mental geography."

E-commerce does not merely master distance, it eliminates it. There is no reason why, under e-commerce, the vendor has to be in any particular place. In fact, the customer as a rule does not know and does not care where the e-commerce vendor is located. And the e-commerce vendor in turn, for example Amazon.com, today the world's biggest bookseller, neither knows nor cares where the purchase order comes from.

If the purchase is itself electronic information—a software program or a trade on a stock market—there is no delivery problem. The "product" itself is, after all, only an entry in a computer memory. It has a legal but no physical existence. (There is, however, a considerable tax problem with this type of trade in electronically delivered goods, which will give the world's tax authorities a headache in 2000. The intelligent ones will drop such taxes, the unintelligent ones will devise nonsense rules of control.)

If the purchase is a book, there is still not much of a

delivery problem. Books ship easily, have high value-to-weight ratios, and pass without much trouble across national boundaries and through customs. But a tractor has to be delivered to where the customer is, and it can neither be delivered electronically nor by parcel post.

Delivery also seems to be needed for newspapers and magazines, that is, for the carriers of printed information. At least, none of the attempts made so far to sell an on-line edition to be read on the subscriber's computer or downloaded from it has been a great success. Subscribers want their paper delivered to the doorstep.

Medical diagnoses and test results are increasingly being put on the Internet. But practically everything to do with sickness care—from the physician's examination to surgery, medication, and physical rehabilitation—has to be delivered where the patient is. And so does all after-purchase service, whether it is servicing a physical product, for example, a machine or a bicycle, or something as nonphysical as a bank loan.

Cars by E-Mail

But at the same time, any business, and indeed any institution, that can organize delivery can operate in any market anywhere, without having any physical presence there.

One example: One of the fastest growing businesses in the United States today is an e-mail seller of new passenger automobiles: CarsDirect.com. Based in a Los Angeles suburb, it was founded as recently as January 1999. CarsDirect.com became in July 1999 one of the twenty largest car dealers in the country, operating in forty of the fifty states of the Union, and selling one thousand vehicles a month. It does not owe its success to cheaper prices or to particular prowess in selling cars; in fact in these areas it still lags well behind such older and bigger e-commerce automobile dealers as Autobytel.com or CarPoint.com, a Microsoft subsidiary. But CarsDirect, unlike its competitors, has organized a unique delivery system. It has signed up eleven hundred traditional dealers throughout the country to deliver CarsDirect's sales to the local purchaser, with a guaranteed delivery date and with quality-controlled service.

Delivery is equally important—it may indeed be more important—in e-commerce between businesses. And by all indications e-commerce between businesses is growing even faster than e-retail commerce and is becoming transnational even faster.

E-commerce separates, for the first time in business history, selling and purchase. Selling is completed when the order has been received and paid for. Purchasing is completed only when the purchase has been delivered and actually not until it satisfies the purchaser's want. And whereas e-commerce demands centralization, delivery has to be totally decentralized. It needs ultimately to be local, detailed, and accurate.

Just as e-commerce separates selling and purchasing, it

separates making and selling. Under e-commerce, what we now know as "production" becomes procurement. There is absolutely no reason at all why any e-commerce facility should limit itself to marketing and selling one maker's products or brands.

In fact, as both Amazon.com and CarsDirect.com show, the great strength of e-commerce is precisely that it provides the customer with a whole range of products, no matter who makes them. But in traditional business structures, selling is still seen and organized as a servant to production, or as the cost center that "sells what we make." In the future, e-commerce companies will "sell what we can deliver."

(2000)

5

The New Economy Isn't Here Yet

This interview was conducted by James Daly, editor in chief of *Business 2.0* magazine, in the author's office in Claremont, California. It was based on the author's specifying the topics and the interviewer's questions. The author himself edited the interviewer's draft into the final text. The interview appeared in the August 12, 2000, issue of *Business 2.0*.

Many of the newer Internet companies are struggling to keep their businesses afloat. What are they doing wrong?

I don't think they are doing anything wrong. They're just not doing anything right. It's highly probable that the age in which you automatically got lots of money by calling yourself a dotcom is over. Many of these Internet start-ups were not start-ups of business, at all. They were just stock exchange gambles. If there was a business plan, it was only to launch an IPO or be bought. Not to build a business. And I am appalled by the greed of to-day's executive.

Is it too late to pull out of the tailspin?

Possibly. Venture capital will be increasingly hard to get for many of them. I once worked with an old financial man. He said that any start-up that promises to have prof-its in less than five years is a phony, but any start-up that doesn't have a positive cash flow in eighteen months is also a phony. Now that may be too orthodox today. The fact that some Internet start-ups take a long time to be-come profitable is fine. Amazon.com is typical. I am not worried about it. But very few of the Internet start-ups will have a positive cash flow ever. And that's not a business.

The argument that many of the start-ups pose is that they are simply buying land while land is cheap. That is, they will spend a lot of money today to build mind-share, and that leads to market share and, ultimately, profitabil-ity in the future.

Okay, but you can only finance mind-share if you have the cash flow. You had exactly the same arguments in the 1920s, although the term *mind-share* didn't exist. *Market share* was also an unknown term. The terms are new, but the illusions or promises are old, and they were the same in all of the other booms. Typically, the speculative boom precedes the growth of the real businesses by ten years. The first great speculative boom of our modern economy was with the railroads. The great English railroad boom in the 1830s led to a collapse of many of the top companies in the early 1840s. After that, railroad building began in earnest. The same happened in this country after the Civil War. The railroad boom was in the 1850s. But railroad building, and profit-making, only began in earnest with the transcontinental railroad after the Civil War.

Does that ten-year beginnings-to-boom timetable still apply? Do you think it will take a decade before we see the real champions of the New Economy emerge?

Yes. The promise in any new business in any new industry is that you have to buy back every penny you spend. But if you don't have the cash flow, you must depend on ever-growing infusions of new money: investment capital. If you don't get what you call mind-share translating into market share, you must depend on stock market gains rather than business gains. And that is very, very risky. It makes you exceedingly vulnerable to even the slightest downturn.

If so, many new Net companies are stock market gambles, what about the established old-line companies? How are they faring on-line?

We all, including myself, greatly underrated the speed at which old businesses have been able to adapt to e-commerce and actually become leaders. Let me give you one example: Four years ago I told one of the world's very large automobile companies they would have to go on the Internet. They listened politely, which means they didn't throw stones at me. But they thought I was absolutely crazy. Now this same company has started an Internet buying collective and is working with at least two, and probably four or five, other big automobile companies. The buying co-op will turn into a worldwide auctions market, and they are moving very aggressively. But it took four years. And they also still only focus on their own brands, instead of being multibrand as the dotcom people are. Both sides still need to learn from each other.

Is it important to be a multibrand organization?

It's critical. If you are, let's say, Ford, and you go on the Internet, you sell Ford cars to Ford dealers. If you're one of the dotcom companies, however, you sell every brand and find the dealer for it. That gives the dotcoms an enormous advantage, but only for the time being. I don't know which of the big automobile companies is going to realize that its marketing strength enables it to become the seller of all brands and especially of the brands that don't have the volume. From all I know, they're all working on it. Give it another six months. They have severe internal problems with these things, however—with dealers, with their own people. They must overcome that.

Are there new metrics for success in an Internet company?

That's a little more than I can answer. A great deal more. But I'm not sure that it will be any different than the traditional metrics. There's an old grand theory of stock market valuation that looks upon the value of a stock as the valuation of future gains. There's a great deal to be said for it. Works very well over fairly long periods of time. And it applies beautifully to the dotcom boom, where the valuation is based on expectations of capital gains. When debt shrinks, the expectations of future earnings become more important and established businesses—but not necessarily large companies only—have a tremendous advantage, because their cost of capital is so much lower. If your cost of capital is based on tremendous stock market gains, then your cost of capital is actually very high if those expectations go down. Still, I do believe that new economics are very badly needed.

Such as? What are the most important numbers you'd look at to value a dotcom?

What I think is irrelevant. What matters is that prospective investors will look on these companies differently and that is very clear.

What do you think the corporation of the future looks like?

Which corporation? What kind of corporation? Interestingly, the impact of the Internet may be much greater on the nonprofits than on for-profit businesses. And on higher education. The cost of your basic resource, brainpower, is going up fast. It has become very expensive. Technically savvy and innovative people have become unbelievably expensive. They can make all the money they want by remaining independent contractors rather than working for one of the companies, no matter what your stock options are.

The impact of the Net on higher education is almost certain to be very much greater than on any business. The average knowledge worker will outlive the average employing organization. This is the first time in history that this has happened. You must have a great deal of knowledge today, and it must often be highly focused. So the center of gravity of higher education is already shifting from the education of the young to the continuing education of adults. Skills in business used to change very slowly. My last name, *drucker,* is Dutch. It means "printer." My ancestors were printers in Amsterdam from 1510 or so until 1750, and during that entire time they didn't have to learn anything new. All of the basic innovations in printing before the nineteenth century had been done by the early sixteenth century. Socrates was a stonemason. If he came back to life and went to work in a stone yard, it would take him about six hours to catch on. Neither the tools nor the products have changed.

Will this ongoing quest for continuing education affect the structure of the corporation?

Almost certainly. The corporation as we know it, which is now 120 years old, is unlikely to survive the next twenty-five years. Legally and financially, yes, but not structurally and economically.

Today's corporation is structured around layers of management. Most of those layers are information relays, and like any relays, they are very poor. Every transfer of information cuts the message in half. There needs to be very few layers of management in the future, and those who relay the information must be very smart. But knowledge, as you know, often becomes obsolete incredibly fast. The continuing professional education of adults is the number one growth industry in the next thirty years, but not in the traditional form. In five years, we will deliver most of our executive management programs on-line. The Internet combines the advantages of both class and book. In a book you can go back to page sixteen. In a class you can't, but in a class there is a physical presence; and on the Internet you have both.

Several years ago you set down the five dos and the three don'ts of innovation. If you were to create those rules for innovation today, what would they be?

Today you need an organization that is a change leader, not just an innovator. Five years ago, you had an enormous amount of literature on creativity. Most of creativity is just hard and systematic work. Fifteen years ago, everyone wanted to be an innovative company, but unless you are a "change leader" company you won't have the mindset for innovation. Innovation has to have a systematic approach. And innovation is very unpredictable. Look, you have a zipper on your pants don't you?

Last time I looked, yes.

No buttons?

No buttons.

But if you look at the invention of the zipper, this is totally irrational. The zipper could not possibly have been a success in the clothing industry. It was invented to close bales of heavy stuff, such as grain, in the port. Nobody thought of clothes. The market turned out to be not where the inventor thought it would be. And this happens time and time again. The first major war fought after the Napoleonic conflicts was the Crimean War of 1854, and it had horrible casualties. It became very important to develop an anesthetic that could be used on the battlefield. One of the first things they came up with was cocaine. It was supposed to be nonaddictive and everyone began using it—Sigmund Freud even. But it was addictive and had to be dropped. Around 1905, a German invented the first nonaddictive anesthetic, called novocaine. The inventor spent the last twenty years of his life trying to get everyone to use it. But where was it used? By dental students. And the inventor could not believe that his noble invention could be used for something as mundane as filling teeth. So the market is almost never where the inventor thinks it will be.

No more than 10 or 15 percent of innovations ever live up to that founder's wishes. Another 15, 20, or 30 percent are not disastrous, but not successes either. Five years later they'll say that this is a nice specialty. You know what that means, don't you? It means you have to wrap it in a bill to give it away. Sixty percent are footnotes at best. Timing is also important. An invention may not succeed, but ten years later someone else does the same thing, gives it a slight twist, and it clicks. Sometimes strategies are more important than the innovation itself. The trouble is that you rarely get a second chance.

Do you believe that an organization should be involved in the process of creative destruction, such as that de-

scribed by Clayton M. Christensen in The Innovator's Dilemma?

Absolutely, but this needs to be an ongoing process and it has to be organized. Let me give you an example of a company that I've worked with. A fairly big one. A leader in a worldwide specialized field. And every three months, a group of people from the organization—younger people, junior people, but never the same people—sits down and looks at one segment of the company's products, or services, or process, or policies with a question: If we didn't do this already, would we go into it the way we are now? And if the answer is no, then the question is, What *would* we do? Every four or five years, that company has systematically abandoned or at least modified every single one of its products and processes, and especially its services. That's the secret of its growth and its profitability.

A company should be able to eliminate its waste. The human body does it automatically. In the corporate body, there is enormous resistance. Abandonment isn't that easy, and don't underrate the effect abandonment can have. It has a tremendous impact on the mind-set of the people and the organization. Sometimes a so-called improvement can become a new product. Of the people and companies I know, 70 percent of the new comes from a slight modification of what already exists. The best example I know is probably GE Medical Electronics. They're a world leader, but not many of their products have come out of innovation. More have come out of improvement.

Any thoughts on the Microsoft antitrust trial?

Antitrust is an obsession of American lawyers, but I have no use for it. Any monopoly holds an umbrella over the newcomers, to be sure, but I am not afraid of monopolies because they eventually collapse. Thucydides wrote years ago that hegemony kills itself. A power that has hegemony always becomes arrogant. Always becomes overweening. And always unites the rest of the world against it. A countervailing power always reacts. A hegemonous system is very self-destructive. It becomes defensive, arrogant, and a defender of yesterday. It destroys itself. Therefore no monopoly in history lives for very long.

The best thing that could happen to an old monopoly is to be broken up. If antitrust had not forced IBM to give up the punch card, it would never have become the computer giant. The best thing that happened to the Rockefellers was to be broken up. The Rockefellers were wedded to kerosene. They considered gasoline a fad. By the time Standard Oil was broken up, it was on the decline. The new companies that were focusing on the growing car market, like Texaco, were growing by leaps and bounds. And five years later, the Rockefeller fortune was ten times what it had been before it was broken up.

So I think the best thing that could happen to Microsoft is to be broken up into several pieces. I do not think Bill Gates would agree with me, but then Mr. Rockefeller did not agree either.

He fought the breaking up of Standard Oil to the very

last minute. AT&T fought it until it became clear that it was hopeless. The same with IBM and old man Watson, whom I knew very well. Not the man who built IBM, but his father, who had the vision of the computer as early as 1929 but when it became a danger to the punch-card business, he did everything to kill the computer. And the antitrust suit enabled his loving sons to ease the old man out. These were clients of mine. Friends of mine.

One of the seminal books that you wrote was The Age of Discontinuity. *If you were to revisit that today, in this age of accelerated change, what would you write?*

I don't know, because I haven't read that book for thirty years. I don't read my old books, I write new ones. But I would put much more emphasis on demographics, much more emphasis on globalization. Much more emphasis on the Internet, particularly on business-to-business e-commerce. What the New Economy or new society will look like you can't predict, but you can see certain trends and some things I believe you can anticipate.

In the last forty or fifty years, economics was dominant. In the next twenty or thirty years, social issues will be dominant. The rapidly growing aging population and the rapidly shrinking younger population means there will be social problems.

Because of manufacturing advances, production will increase exponentially. But manufacturing employment is disappearing. Blue-collar employment and the share of manufacturing in gross national product are going down. We came out of World War II with farming still employing

25 percent of the workforce, and producing some 20 percent of the gross national product. It is down to 3 and 5 percent now. And manufacturing moves in the same direction, but maybe not going that far down. If you translate manufacturing goods prices into stable dollars, they have been going down at least 1 to 2 percent a year since 1960.

How does one manage successfully in this time of dramatic change?

It is very tempting to manage only for the short term, but very dangerous. One of the things managers have to learn, and very few of them have, is to balance short term and long term. I would say the unique accomplishment of CEO Jack Welch of GE has been that he has been developing the tools for keeping an eye on the financial short term—and by that I don't mean six months but three years—but he has a very strong emphasis on developing people long term. Call it a mind power strategy. This came fairly easy to GE because GE in the 1920s developed a sound and modern financial strategy, and it was one of the very first companies in the 1930s to develop a human resources strategy. So these are all GE traditions. Jack Welch has put this balance to the forefront of his business. He gets monthly reports on each of his 167 businesses, I am sure, but he makes people investments for seven years ahead.

How do you turn transition to an advantage?

By looking at every change, looking out every window. And asking: Could this be an opportunity? Is this new thing a genuine change, or simply a fad? And the difference is very simple: A change is something people do, and a fad is something people talk about. An enormous amount of talk is a fad. I have an old friend and he is an important man at a big institution. I think he was being accused of never changing anything. He has a very prosperous, very successful organization, and he said buying a book about change is much cheaper than changing anything. You must also ask yourself if these transitions, these changes, are an opportunity or a threat. If you start out by looking at change as threat, you will never innovate. Don't dismiss something simply because this is not what you had planned. The unexpected is often the best source of innovation.

Remember that many transitions may be meaningless for a particular business. They may be exceedingly meaningful for some other institution, but for us they are meaningless. They don't change our market, they don't change our customers, they don't change our technology, and the large part is just things they talk about at conferences. So most of the things are not for us. You may read about these changes. It's very interesting and I put a sticker on it and have all of my people read it. And they discuss it. And I will remember it, and five years later, yes, maybe I do something. It becomes part of my instrument kit. So you just watch out at every window.

What do you believe is the future of business on the Internet?

I think it's too early to speculate about e-commerce.

One never knows how a new distribution channel will change what is being distributed and how customer values will change. If e-commerce takes even only a relatively small part of the total consumer business (and it may take a fairly large part), it will have a profound impact and force existing distribution channels to change radically.

I think one high-probability guess is a system that uses e-commerce to sell and a physical location to deliver. That is already being developed very rapidly in Japan. Ito-Yokado is probably the world's largest retailer today. And they own, among other things, the Japanese 7-Eleven stores. Japan has ten thousand 7-Elevens. Increasingly, they have deals with all kinds of suppliers where customers buy on-line and pick up at the nearest 7-Eleven. Because a central problem of e-commerce is delivery.

The delivery has to be local. That is fairly easy if you sell books. Books have an enormously high value-to-weight ratio. There is almost no product except diamonds that has a ratio as high. They are very easily shipped, and true, they can be damaged, but they're fairly sturdy. All over the world transportation costs of books are artificially low. They are subsidized heavily. In this country, the best guess is that it costs the post office four times what it charges. So books are easy, but tractors aren't quite that easy. And perishables are hopeless. So I would say there is high probability that you will see develop a system in which selling is on-line and delivery is in a physical location. At Japanese 7-Elevens, the on-line pickup system already accounts for about 40 percent of what the store sells. The 7-Eleven gets a small commission but it costs them nothing, it's pure gravy. So I think that is one of the likely things. Other changes are also profound. Because for the first time selling, making, and delivery are separated. The center of power has been shifting to distribution now for fifty years. That's accelerated by several orders of magnitude. How many manufacturing plants will survive? Not many. But so far the distributor has squandered that power. The distributors already have the brands, but only a very few of the very big manufacturers have brands that have real standing in the consumer market.

In other areas, the design of a product, its manufacture, marketing, and servicing will become separate businesses. They may be owned by the same financial control but basically run as separate businesses. Ford is considered a manufacturing company, but they manufacture very little. They assemble. Which is a radical break with the mass-production concept. So the changes are very profound and very deep and very long lasting. And we are just beginning to understand what it all means.

(2000)

6

The CEO in the New Millennium

A few years ago, as we all remember, there was a great deal of talk about the "end of hierarchy." We would all be one big happy crew, sailing together on the same ship. Well, it hasn't happened and it isn't about to happen, for one simple reason: When the ship is going down, you don't call a caucus—you give a command. There has to be somebody who says, "Enough dithering—this is it." Without a decision maker, you'll never make a decision. Moreover, as our corporate institutions become increasingly complex—technologically, economically, and socially—the more we need to know just who the ultimate authority is. So instead of discussing the disappearance or the weakening of top management, I want to focus on the new demands facing it.

If we take a look at the position of the CEO over the next fifteen years or so, there are five key points that I think stand out—all interrelated but also quite separate. What are these points, and precisely how will they affect an executive's career?

Transforming Governance

I am absolutely certain that fifteen years from now the governance of corporations will be substantially different from the present. The reason I can be so sure is that we are seeing a fundamental change in the corporate owner-ship structure, and this invariably goes hand in hand with changes in governance.

Today, particularly in developed countries, financial considerations are ultimately driving ownership interests. We can look at our aging population as one example. The population of the United States is now growing older. As a result, more people are worrying about their future fi-nancial resources. This boosts the importance of pension funds—how and where they are invested. Issues such as these influence the makeup and concerns of corporate owners. It's reasonable, I think, to say that the institutional investor as the decisive owner is here to stay.

What does that mean for the governance of the cor-poration—and for the CEO? There's an enormous chal-lenge ahead to educate the new owners, many of whom, as I've noted, are financial people. I once was a securities analyst, so that gives me license to say that it is virtually impossible to make a financial person understand business. I am not being facetious. Financial people don't deal with the issue of balance between often conflicting elements—short versus long term, continuity versus change, improving today versus creating tomorrow. Corporate leaders who wrestle with these issues every day know the amount of struggle involved, but it's difficult for financial people to understand this. Of course, these new owners have their own issues and pressures to deal with, not the least of which include the American pension system and how to increase corporate profits.

One of the most critical jobs ahead for CEOs will be to think this all through in relation to their particular business and come up with ways to strike reasonable balances. Executives who have experience in attaining corporate balance usually find that they have a pretty good feel for what needs to be done, even when it isn't easy to do and even though they may make mistakes. But the worst mistake is trying to avoid the issue of governance. Many people I know try to duck the issue, hiding behind the misguided mantra of "We are running this place for the short-term interest of the shareholder."

I think we are getting to the end of that. Today's leaders have to accept the fact that the interest of the shareholder as expressed in yesterday's Dow Jones Industrial Average is not what they are running the company by. Not only governance, but its related concepts and tools, will need to be confronted and transformed over the next fifteen years. And not only in the United States. There is no country today that can claim current success with corporate governance. It doesn't work anymore in Germany and it doesn't work anymore in Japan. Ownership structure has fundamentally, dramatically, permanently changed—everywhere.

Many executives have already begun to tackle the governance issue. They have found that it isn't easy, but neither is it impossible. Those executives who haven't yet faced this challenge will find that they have little choice but to do so over the next decade.

New Approaches to Information

We have heard endlessly that we are living in an Information Revolution, and indeed we are. Forty years ago when the computer first came out, most people saw it as an extremely fast adding machine. A few of us, however, took it more seriously and saw it as a new way to process information. We were convinced that within twenty to thirty years, new information would transform the job of running the business.

But, so far, except perhaps for the military, our new information capacities have had practically no impact on the way we run businesses. Where we have seen a tremendous impact is on the way we run operations.

Two examples: My grandson, who is completing his

internship in architecture, recently showed me the software he is using to complete his final thesis—a project for a large architecture firm. This firm put in a bid to design the heating, lighting, and plumbing for a new prison building. The software my grandson showed me can, literally in the twinkling of an eye, do work that once took hundreds of individuals to complete. Meanwhile, in medical schools and teaching hospitals, virtual reality presentations are providing a new and effective way to train surgeons. Up until now, surgeons would not actually see surgical operations until their final year of residency—before then, they would see only the back of the surgeon who was performing the operation. Today, young surgeons can actually do what is essential to learning surgical techniques—practice—and with virtual reality they can do this without endangering the well-being of patients.

In businesses across the board, information technology has had an obvious impact. But until now that impact has been only on concrete elements—not intangibles like strategy and innovation. Thus, for the CEO, new information has had little impact on how he or she makes decisions. That is going to have to change.

Let's take two positions most CEOs are familiar with. Today, practically every corporation has a chief financial officer, to whom the accounting department reports. This is our oldest information system; in many ways it's obsolete, but companies cling to accounting because it's what they understand—it's familiar. Likewise many companies

have a management information systems officer, or chief information officer, who presides over a computer system that is generally enormously expensive.

But neither of these officers knows one blessed thing about information. They understand data, and within fifteen years, the two will be under one manager and both will be different. The changes currently under way in accounting are the most substantive since the 1920s. They include activity-based accounting and economic-chain accounting and so on. Essentially, we are changing basic record-keeping to accommodate present economic reality— something accounting was never designed to do. At the same time, we are merging this with our data-producing capacity, so you will have an information system that will look very different. And yet it will not give the CEO the information he or she needs most: what goes on outside the enterprise.

One of the biggest mistakes I have made during my career was coining the term *profit center,* around 1945. The truth is that inside the business, there are only cost centers. The only profit center is a customer whose check hasn't bounced. We know literally nothing about the outside, and yet, even if you are the leading business in an industry, the great majority of the people who buy your kind of product or services are not your customers. If you have 30 percent of the market, you are the giant. But that means that 70 percent of the customers do not buy your product or your services, and we know nothing about them.

These "noncustomers" are particularly important because they represent a source of information that can help you gauge the changes that will affect your industry. How so? If you look at the changes in major industries over the last forty years, you'll see that practically all of them occurred outside the existing market, or product, or technology. Whatever the business, senior people need to spend more time outside their own shop. There is no question that getting to know your noncustomers is far from easy, but it really is the only way to expand your knowledge. The people I know, for example, who have been successful building their business in Japan made a point of studying Japanese history before making contact. We are fortunate in the United States because of our cultural diversity and we should use that asset to our advantage.

In the nineteenth century, you could take for granted that each major industry spawned a specific technology, and that technologies from separate industries would never meet. This is the hypothesis on which all the great research labs have been founded, beginning with Siemens in Germany in 1869. That assumption no longer works. Technologies now crisscross each other all the time, and productivity is no guarantee of achievement. In the last thirty years, Bell Laboratories has been more productive than at any other time in its history—but what is its track record during this period for major technological breakthroughs?

There is no question that businesses need to understand what goes on outside their spheres. But so far there is almost no information—and what little exists is at best anecdotal. We're only beginning to learn how to quantify this information. So far, whenever anyone claims to have done so, I know that somebody has put a thumb on the scale.

Command and Control

Closely allied to this is another factor—less and less work is being done in the traditional way, in which companies (especially large ones) try to control everything they need and do within a defined power sphere. I am not necessarily happy about how this is coming about. People talk glibly about the disappearance of command and control. Yes, but what is taking its place? We see a growing number of companies working with contractors and temps, a rise in the number of joint ventures, a growth in outsourcing— all kinds of liaisons. Many of the people who work for a company are probably not its employees, and one prediction I've heard is that in a few years the people who are not employees of the organization for which they work, including government, will greatly exceed the number who are.

One sign that this is happening is the explosive growth of the experts, the management consultants. I once promised *Harvard Business Review* an article on the management consultant, a sort of user's guide (something CEOs are sorely in need of). I couldn't do it. There is just too much going on. In my view, this is a sign that more and more of the input we need will not be from people or organizations that we control, but from people and organizations with which we have a relationship, a partnership—people whom we cannot command.

Successful participants in joint ventures understand that one can't "command" one's partner. Working with a partner is essentially a marketing job, and that means asking questions: What are the other party's values? Objectives? Expectations? But of course there are times when command is critical to getting things done. The CEO of tomorrow will have to be able to understand when to command and when to partner. This is not without precedent—J. P. Morgan built a partnership of twelve people, yet he still knew when to assume the role of leader—but it won't be effortless.

The Rise of Knowledge Work

What is going to be the one and only comparative advantage a developed country will have tomorrow? One lesson we have all learned, in part from our experience during the two World Wars, is how to train people almost overnight.

Shortly after the end of the Korean War, I was sent to Korea. The country had experienced far more destruction than either Germany or Japan had in World War II. Moreover, for fifty years preceding the war, the Japanese had not allowed any higher education in Korea. Yet, with the proper support and training, it took less than ten years to convert a purely rural (and primitively so, at that) labor force into a highly productive one.

You can no longer depend on the competitive advantage of knowledge. Technology travels incredibly fast. The only real advantage the United States has—perhaps for the next thirty or forty years—is a substantial supply of something that is not easily created overnight: knowledge workers. In the United States, there are 12 million college students. In China, the top students are extremely well trained, but there are only 1.5 million college students out of a population of 1.2 billion. If we had the same ratio in the United States, we would have just 250,000 college students. Now, we can argue that we may have a few too many, especially in the law schools, but still, the productivity of knowledge work and knowledge workers is visible. The trouble is that we haven't worked on it.

Today's knowledge workers are probably less productive than in the past because their schedules are filled with activities that don't reflect their training or talent. The best-trained people in the world are American nurses. Yet whenever we make a study on nurses, we find that 80 percent of their time is spent on things they aren't trained for. They spend time filling out papers for which nobody apparently has any need. No one knows what happens to those papers, but they have to be filled out nonetheless and the task falls to the nurses. In department stores, salespeople spend 70 to 80 percent of their time serving not the customer but the computer. How to make the knowledge worker more appropriately productive is a challenge we will need to face seriously over the next twenty years.

With manual work, we start with the question "How do you do the work?" You take this work for granted. In knowledge work, you start with the questions "What do you do and what should you be doing?" Answering these questions is critical if we want to maintain our competitive advantage. Physical resources no longer provide much of an advantage, nor does skill. Only the productivity of knowledge workers makes a measurable difference—and right now it is quite poor.

Tying It Together

What does all this really mean? First, it means that the CEO's job is to set a clear direction of what his or her company means by "results." It means that the CEO needs to provide a clear understanding of when it is time to push here and pull back there—and when it's time to abandon something. Tomorrow's leader won't be able to lead by charisma. He or she will need to think through the fundamentals so that other people can work productively.

This will be quite demanding, especially considering the speed of change, the expectations of the new workforce, and an increasingly competitive world economy. But it will also be demanding because it is no longer adequate to have a policy and expect it to carry you through the years. Some companies, such as General Motors, AT&T, and Sears, have had success with long-term major policies. But they are the exceptions; the truth is that ten years is common. Now the changes are coming so fast that changes every three to four years will likely become commonplace.

Increasingly, a CEO's job will be much more like the most complex job I know, which is running an opera. You have your stars and you can't give them orders; you have the supporting cast and the orchestra; you have the people who work behind the scenes; and you have your audience. Each group is completely different. But the opera conductor has a score, and everybody has the same score. In a business you have to make sure all the various groups converge to produce the desired result. This is the key to understanding what's ahead. It's not about being less or more important, but differently important. It's not about refraining from giving orders—but knowing when to give an order and when to treat someone like a partner. And it is not, I assure you, about playing down financial objectives; on the contrary, our demographics tell us that this will become more important. But you will have to know how to integrate your financial objectives with the need to build and maintain a business.

(1997)

Part II

BUSINESS OPPORTUNITIES

7

Entrepreneurs and Innovation

This interview was conducted by George Gendron, editor in chief of *Inc.* magazine, in the author's office in Claremont, California. It was based on the author's specifying the topics and the interviewer's questions. The author himself edited the interviewer's draft into the final text. The interview appeared in a special 1996 issue in *Inc.* magazine.

Do you agree that we in the United States are the best practitioners of entrepreneurship, that we're way ahead of other countries?

Absolutely not! It's a delusion, and a dangerous one. We may have the largest number of new-business starts and new-business failures, but that's all. We're probably not even number two.

Who's number one?

Undoubtedly Korea. Barely forty years ago, Korea had no industry at all. The Japanese, who had ruled Korea for decades, didn't allow any. They also didn't allow any higher education, so there were practically no educated people in Korea. By the end of the Korean War, South Korea had been destroyed. Today Korea is world-class in two dozen industries and the world's leader in shipbuilding and other areas.

If Korea is number one, and we're not number two, who is?

Not too far behind Korea is Taiwan, which like Korea was preindustrial in 1950. Today Taiwan is a world leader in a number of high-tech areas, including microchips. And don't forget the Chinese, who are starting new business after new business on both sides of the Pacific.

Okay, so third is still respectable, no?

The U.S. record is no better than Japan's or Germany's. Japan has a larger proportion of world-class companies that either didn't exist forty years ago or were mom-and-pop shops: Sony, Honda, Yamaha, Kyocera, Matsushita, for example.

Germany owes its rise from the ashes of World War II to its present position—the world's third-largest economy and number one in per capita exports of manufactured goods—to an explosion of entrepreneurship that turned hundreds of brand-new or obscure little shops into world-class manufacturers and industry leaders.

One example is Bertelsmann, one of the world's largest

multimedia companies, which is active in forty countries. In 1946, when Reinhard Mohn, the great-grandson of the founder, returned from a prisoner-of-war camp, Bertels-mann was a small-town publisher of religious tracts.

You said a moment ago that America's entrepreneurial "delusion" is dangerous. How so?

What bothers me more than the fact that the common belief in our entrepreneurial superiority simply isn't true is that it's lulling us into a dangerous complacency—not unlike our complacency about management in the early 1970s. Then we were convinced that American manage-ment reigned supreme, just as the Japanese were about to run circles around us in mass production and customer service.

I'm afraid our complacency about our entrepreneurship and innovation is going to have us outflanked again, not only by the Japanese but also by the Koreans.

Why do you think this is happening?

In this country we by and large still believe that entre-preneurship is having a great idea and that innovation is largely R&D, which is technical. Of course we *know* that entrepreneurship is a discipline, a fairly rigorous one, and that *innovation* is an economic not a technical term, and entrepreneurship creates a new business. That's not news. In fact, it's what made Edison so successful more than a century ago. But American businesses with few excep-tions—Merck, Intel, and Citibank come to mind—still seem to think that innovation is a "flash of genius," not a systematic, organized, rigorous discipline.

The Japanese are organizing innovation. So are the Koreans. They've set up small groups of their brightest people to systematically apply the discipline of innovation to identify and develop new business.

Is there any one key to that discipline?

Innovation requires us to systematically identify changes that have already occurred in the business—in demographics, in values, in technology or science—and then to look at them as opportunities. It also requires something that is most difficult for existing companies to do: to abandon rather than defend yesterday.

The Four Entrepreneurial Pitfalls

So many new businesses start out with high promise. They do extremely well the first year or two and then suddenly are up to their ears in trouble. If they survive at all, they are forever stunted. Are there typical mistakes entrepreneurs make but could avoid?

There are actually four points—I call them *entrepreneurial pitfalls*—where the new and growing business typically gets into trouble. All four are foreseeable and avoidable.

The first comes when the entrepreneur has to face the fact that the new product or service is not successful where he or she thought it would be but is successful in a totally different market. Many businesses disappear because the founder-entrepreneur insists that he or she knows better than the market.

So, often the entrepreneur is actually succeeding but doesn't realize it?

No, it's worse than that. He or she rejects success. You want examples? There are thousands of them, but one of the best is over one hundred years old.

A man by the name of John Wesley Hyatt had invented the roller bearing. He made up his mind that it was just right for the axles of railroad freight cars. Railroads traditionally stuffed the wheels of their cars with rags soaked in oil to handle the friction. The railroads, however, were not ready for radical change; they liked their rags. And Mr. Hyatt went bankrupt trying to persuade them otherwise.

When Alfred Sloan, the man who later built GM, graduated from MIT at the head of his class in the mid-1890s, he asked his father to buy him Hyatt's small bankrupt business. Unlike Hyatt, Sloan was willing to broaden his vision of the product. It turned out that the roller bearing was ideal for the automobile, which was just coming to market. In two years Sloan had a flourishing business; for twenty years Henry Ford was his biggest customer.

Good story, but is the rejection of success really all that common?

I'd say that the majority of successful new inventions or products don't succeed in the market for which they were originally designed. I've seen it again and again.

Novocaine was invented in 1905 by German chemist Alfred Einhorn for use in major surgery, but it wasn't suitable. Dentists immediately wanted the product, but the inventor actually tried to stop them from using it for the "mundane purpose" of drilling teeth. To the end of his days, Einhorn traveled all over the world preaching the merits of novocaine as a general anesthetic.

More recently, I know of a company whose founder created a software program that he was absolutely sure was what every hospital needed to operate smoothly. Well, the hospitals told him they weren't organized the way he assumed. He didn't make a single sale to a hospital. By pure accident, though, a small city stumbled over the program and found it was just what it needed. Orders began to come in from medium-size cities around the country. And he refused to fill them.

Why do entrepreneurs reject unexpected success?

Because it's not what they had planned. Entrepreneurs believe that they are in control. That leads to pitfall number two. Entrepreneurs believe that profit is what matters most in a new enterprise. But profit is secondary. Cash flow matters most.

Growing bodies need to be fed, and a business that grows fast devours cash. You have to make constant investments just to keep even. This is totally predictable, so getting caught in a cash crunch is totally unnecessary. I have saved more new enterprises than I can remember by simply telling the founder who showed me how beautifully things were going that *now* is the time to provide for your next financing. If you have six months' to a year's time to provide for your next financing, you can be reasonably sure you'll get it and at favorable terms.

Why do you think entrepreneurs have such a hard time grasping the concept of cash flow?

They're not the only ones. Warren Buffet once said that if he wants to find out how a company is doing, he doesn't listen to security analysts. They talk profit, which is irrelevant. He listens to bank credit analysts; they talk cash flow. I have yet to see one of the stock market newsletters I get talk about liquidity and the financial position of a growing company. They talk about profit margins and profitability.

Why is that? Is it a product of our business schools?

No. Fundamentally, businesspeople are financially illiterate.

Well, let's say the business pays attention to cash flow, gets beyond the cash crunch, and grows rapidly beyond expectations. What's the third pitfall looming on the horizon?

When the business grows, the person who founded it is incredibly busy. Rapid growth puts an enormous strain on a business. You outgrow your production facilities. You outgrow your management capabilities.

The entrepreneur begins running around like the proverbial one-armed paperhanger. He sees the sales figures, and he sees profit forecasts. Those make him believe that in another year he can sell out and get $10 million. And he doesn't see that he's outgrowing his management base.

You know, I've worked with entrepreneurs for fifty years and can say that there is a fairly normal curve; 80 percent fall within it. Even if your business is growing at a normal rate—not tripling in size every six months, but growing at a good, solid, sustainable rate—the management crunch hits you at the end of the fourth year.

That's when you outgrow your management base?

Yes. Starting out, the typical founder does everything himself. He has helpers, but he doesn't have colleagues. Then suddenly everything goes wrong. The quality falls out of bed. Customers don't pay. Deliveries are missed.

But every young business makes mistakes, lots of them. What's the one symptom an entrepreneur cannot afford to ignore when it comes to outgrowing management?

I always ask people who come to me how they respond to opportunity. "Suppose a customer says, 'If you make ten thousand of product X, we'll give you a contract.' Do you see this as a burden or an opportunity?" When they say, "Of course it's an opportunity, but I'm worried about it because it's an extra burden," I say, "Look, my friend, you've outgrown your management base."

To avoid a crisis, you should sit down and create a management team. By that time you have maybe forty people working for you. Look them over to see who shows management ability. You call in those four or five people (you're not likely to have more), and you say, "I want each of you to sit down alone next weekend and look at the other people here, including me. Don't look at yourself. Look at the others, and think about what each of them is good at." And then you all sit down together, take a fresh sheet of paper, and list the key activities of the business. Today we call this "establishing our core competencies."

Young entrepreneurs can't pay to bring in a management team. But here's Tom, and Tom is good at customer service, so you might also let him run the office. Give him an extra load for a few months or a few years, or give him an assistant. But Tom's job now is customer service. And here's Jane, your manufacturing person, who's better than anybody else at handling people. So your manufacturing person also becomes your people person.

And you start to meet once a month, maybe on a Saturday, and within a year you have a management team. It takes at least a year, more likely eighteen months, to create a team.

To really begin to work together as a team?

Yes, but also to know that even though Joe's a difficult person to work with, he's exactly the financial person we need. Or to know that Tom is developing into a first-rate sales and marketing manager but is a weak customer-service manager. Tom may have been the best you had, but he ain't good enough.

That's a hard decision for an entrepreneur to make, especially if Tom was there at the start.

Yes, but if you start to build your team eighteen months ahead of time, Tom's going to know that it's time to step aside. You can't wait until everything falls out of bed at the same time.

And the fourth pitfall?

The fourth pitfall is the most difficult one. It's when the business is a success, and the entrepreneur begins to put himself before the business. Here is a person who's worked eighteen hours a day for fourteen years and has a $60-million business and a management team that works. Now he asks himself, "What do I want to do? What's my role?" Those are the wrong questions. If you start out with them, you invariably end up killing yourself and the business.

What should you be asking?

You should be asking, "What does the *business* need at this stage?" The next question is "Do I have those qualities?"

You have to start with what the business needs. That's where an outsider can be very helpful.

Over the years I've had maybe one hundred people come to me in that situation. And when I ask them why they've come to me, most say that their wife says that they're not doing a good job anymore, that they're destroying themselves, their family, and the business. Occasionally you have a bright daughter who says it. If the son says it, he's brushed aside by the founder, who's thinking, Does he want to take over and push me out? But a wife or a bright daughter can say that.

Sometimes an outside shareholder speaks up, or an accountant or a lawyer. Usually somebody has to kick that entrepreneur hard to get him to face up to the harsh reality that he doesn't enjoy this anymore. He knows he's not concentrating on the right things.

Do you think entrepreneurs today are smarter about avoiding the pitfalls you've been describing?

No.

No? With all the education, with all the MBAs?

No. Education gives you neither experience nor wisdom.

Can Large Companies Foster Entrepreneurship?

Back in the 1980s we heard a lot about "intrapreneurship," but it all seemed very faddish. Now that the hype has died down, can large companies really foster entrepreneurship?

Of course it's possible. Quite a few do it. And many midsize companies are even better at it. But it's different from what most books mean by the term *entrepreneurship*. Most books take their cue from the last great entrepreneurial period in Western history before ours—the sixty years before World War I. All our major institutions, not just our business institutions, were created and shaped in that period.

The period began with the Great Exhibition, in London, in 1851, which ushered in the Second Industrial Revolution. The 1850s saw William Henry Perkin, in England, invent the first aniline dye and with it the modern chemical industry.

That was the decade that saw Werner von Siemens, in Germany, invent the first electric motor and with it the modern electrical industry. That was the decade that saw the triumph of Cyrus McCormick's reaper and with it the invention of mechanized agriculture. That was the decade that brought the first transatlantic cable and the first regular transatlantic steamship service. That was the decade in which Bessemer, in England, invented the steelmaking process, and the brothers Pereire, in France, founded the Crédit Mobilier and with it modern finance.

From that point until 1914, we had a major new invention every fourteen months or so, each immediately creating a new industry.

How was that period of innovation different from today's?

All those new industries moved into a vacuum. There were no large corporations when the railroad in this country became one. And there was no competition. The railroad didn't displace anybody, didn't cause any dislocation. But now the world is full of organizations. And we're in turmoil because so many of the organizations whose roots go back one hundred years or more are not going to survive.

What does that mean for entrepreneurship in large companies?

The large organization has to learn to innovate, or it

won't survive. For some companies that means reinventing themselves. Increasingly, large companies are growing through alliances and joint ventures. Yet very few of the big boys know how to manage an alliance. They're used to giving orders, not to working with a partner, and it's totally different. In an alliance or a joint venture, you have to begin by asking, "What do our partners want? What are our shared values and goals?" Those aren't easy questions for somebody who grew up at GE or Citibank and is now at the top or near the top of a huge worldwide enterprise.

But innovation also means changing your products and services to keep up with markets that are changing faster than anybody has ever seen. Look at what's happening with banks. There are only a few large banks today in this country that make a profit out of doing the things banks traditionally do—commercial loans or deposits, for example. Banks are making profits out of credit cards, ATM fees, currency trades, and mutual fund sales. To stay in business, the large organization has to innovate.

But can large companies foster entrepreneurship?

They have to, to compensate for the difficulty they usually have learning how to work in a partnership or alliance. What do they do? They set up a unit internally that behaves quite differently from the rest of the company. The more successful the unit, the more difficult it is to make sure that the large company doesn't put the same expectations on it as it does for the rest of the company.

When it's a new venture, whether it's outside or inside the business, it's a child. And you don't put a forty-pound pack on a six-year-old's back when you take her hiking.

What are some examples of companies that have been successful at internal entrepreneurship?

There are companies that are good at improving what they're already doing; the Japanese call this *kaizen*. There are companies that are good at extending what they're doing. And finally there are companies that are good at innovation. Every large company has to be able to do all three—*improve, extend, and innovate*—simultaneously. I don't know of any large companies that can do that yet. But they're learning.

The Rise of Social Entrepreneurship

Could you step back and summarize your views about social entrepreneurship?

First, it's as important as economic entrepreneurship. More important, perhaps. In the United States, we have a very healthy economy but a very sick society. So perhaps social entrepreneurship is what we need the most—in health care, education, city government, and so on. Fortunately there are enough successes around so that we know it can be done—and also how to do it.

For instance?

You have to start small—the big cure-alls never work. That was the problem with President Clinton's health care reform plan. Now we are experimenting in health care all over the lot, and the outline of a new American health care system is slowly emerging out of literally hundreds of local experiments. We still talk about big, ambitious, nationwide educational cure-alls, yet in a lot of places *local* schools—public, parochial, *and* private—are having successes based on *local* entrepreneurs. And we know that the American public—especially the young, educated, double-earner family—is ready to support social entrepreneurship, especially as volunteers.

You've said that more and more community jobs are being handled by local institutions, for-profits and nonprofits. Why are so many small nonprofits, to use your phrase, "grotesquely mismanaged"?

Because they wrongly believe that good intentions move mountains. Bulldozers move mountains. But there are exceptions.

I helped start a foundation for nonprofit management in 1990. We have in our files more than one thousand stories of small and mostly local institutions that do a job that nobody else can do. We gave our annual innovation award this year to the Rainforest Alliance, which has found a way to save the rain forest while increasing both the crop and the income of the banana farmers, once the greatest enemy of the rain forest. Even the runners-up for the award are social innovators.

These are social entrepreneurs, not business entrepreneurs. The social entrepreneur changes the performance capacity of society. Clearly the need is there, or we wouldn't have founded eight hundred thousand nonprofits over the past thirty years.

Yesterday *charity* meant writing out a check. Today more and more people who are reasonably successful don't feel that's enough. They are looking for a parallel career, not a second career. Very few of them change jobs.

You've said that you think we're on the verge of a period of enormous innovation. We've also got enormous numbers of people in the private sector who want to be involved in social entrepreneurship. Are you arguing that we're now going to see more social innovation than we've seen in a long time?

No doubt about it.

But so many people in business are leery of nonprofits because they see them as nonprofessional.

And they're both right and wrong. They're right because far too many nonprofits are either poorly managed or not managed at all. But they're wrong because nonprofits are not businesses and should be run differently.

In what way?

They need more not less management, precisely because they don't have a financial bottom line. Both their mission and their "product" have to be clearly defined and continually assessed. And most have to learn how to attract and hold volunteers whose satisfaction is measured in responsibility and accomplishment, not wages.

What about innovation and entrepreneurship in government?

That's probably our most important challenge. Look, no government in any major developed country really works anymore. The United States, the United Kingdom, Germany, France, Japan—none has a government the citizens respect or trust.

In every country there's a cry for leadership. But it's the wrong cry. When you have a malfunction across the spectrum, you don't have a people problem, you have a systems problem.

Modern government needs innovation. What we have now is roughly four hundred years old. The invention of the nation-state and of modern government in the closing years of the sixteenth century was certainly one of the most successful innovations ever. Within two hundred years they conquered the globe.

But it's time for new thinking. The same holds true for the economic theories that have dominated the past sixty years or so. Government—not businesses or nonprofits— is going to be the most important area of entrepreneurship and innovation over the next twenty-five years.

(1996)

8

They're Not Employees, They're People

Every working day, the world's biggest nongovernmental employer, the Swiss company Adecco, places 700,000 of its employees as "temporaries" with businesses all over the world—perhaps as many as 250,000 in the United States. Adecco is the industry giant, but it has only a small share of a totally splintered market. In the United States alone there are some seven thousand temp firms. Together they place some 2.5 million workers each day. And worldwide the figure is at least 8 million, if not 10 million. And 70 percent of all "temps" work full-time.

When the temp industry first started, some fifty years ago, it supplied low-level clerks to take the place of ledger keepers, receptionists, telephone operators, or stenos in the typing pool who were sick or on vacation. Today there are temp suppliers for every job, all the way up to temp CEOs. One temp firm, for instance, supplies manufacturing managers who are in charge of a new plant from its inception on the drawing board until it is in full production. Another supplies highly skilled health-care professionals such as nurse anesthesiologists.

In a related but distinct development, the fastest-growing business service in the United States during the 1990s was the professional employer organization (PEO). There are now at least eighteen hundred of them with their own trade association (The National Organization of Professional Employer Organizations) and their own monthly journal *(The PeoEmp Journal).* These firms manage their clients' employees and their clients' employee relations as well. Virtually unknown only ten years ago, they had become by the year 2000 the "coemployers" of 2.5 to 3 million American employees, both blue collar and white collar.

PEOs, like temp agencies, have vastly expanded their scope in recent years. The first PEOs in the late 1980s offered to do bookkeeping, especially payroll, for their clients. Now PEOs take care of every task in employment management and employee relations: record keeping and legal compliance; hiring, training, placement, promotion, firing, and layoffs; retirement plans and pension payments. They originally confined themselves to taking care of the employee relations of small firms. But Exult (headquartered in Irvine, California)—probably the best known of them—was designed from its start in 1997 to be the coemployer for Fortune 500 companies. It numbers among its clients BP Amoco—worldwide—Unisys, and Tenneco Automotive. It has already gone public and is traded on NASDAQ. In one quarter—the second quarter of 2001— its revenues grew from $43.5 million to $64.3 million. Another PEO, designed originally to do payroll for small businesses with fewer than twenty employees, is about to take over the management of the 120,000 employees of one of the larger states. And some other large firms are getting into the act—e.g., Accenture (the former Andersen Consulting).

But who is then the "boss" of these outsourced employees? If the PEO makes the hiring, firing, placement, and promotion decisions, how can an executive function? I asked this question of a senior BP Amoco executive whose workforce, including senior scientists, is now being managed by Exult. His answer: "Exult knows that it has to satisfy my colleagues and me if it wants to keep the contract. But Exult makes the decisions to fire or to move someone. It does so however only because I suggested it or after careful consultation with me. But I also know that Exult has *three* obligations—to me, to the company, and to the employee—and if it does not satisfy the employee, he or she will leave. And so, in one or two cases, I have yielded when Exult argued that moving an employee I very much would have liked to keep was in the employee's best interest—and probably, long term, in that of the company as well."

Both the temp industry and the PEOs are growing fast.

Adecco is growing 15 percent a year. The PEO industry is growing even faster, 30 percent a year—in other words, it is doubling every two and a half years. It expects to be the coemployer of 10 million American workers by the year 2005.

Clearly, something is happening in employee relations and employee management that does not fit what the management books still write about and what we teach in management school. And it surely also does not fit with the way human relations departments of most organizations—businesses, governments, and nonprofits—were designed and are meant to function.

Strangled in Red Tape

The reason usually offered for the popularity of temps is that they give employers flexibility. But far too many temps work for the same employer for long periods of time—sometimes year after year—for it to be the whole explanation. And flexibility surely does not explain the emergence of the PEOs. A more plausible explanation is that both types of organization legally make "nonemployees" out of people who work for a business. The driving force behind both the steady growth of temps and the emergence of the PEOs is the growing burden of rules and regulations for employers.

The cost alone of these rules and regulations threatens

to strangle small businesses. According to the government's Small Business Administration, the annual cost of government regulations, government-required paperwork, and tax compliance for U.S. businesses employing fewer than five hundred employees was $5,000 per employee in 1995 (the last year for which figures are available)—a 25 percent surcharge on top of the cost of wages, health care, insurance, and pension, which was around $22,500 in 1995 for the average small-business employee. Since then the cost of employment-related paperwork is estimated to have gone up by more than 10 percent.

Many of these costs can be avoided altogether by using temporary workers in place of employees. That's why so many companies are contracting for workers with temp agencies—even though the hourly cost of a temp is often substantially higher than the wage-and-benefit cost of an employee. Another way to reduce the bureaucratic costs is to outsource employee relations—in other words, to let a specialist do the paperwork. Aggregating enough small businesses to manage at least five hundred employees as one workforce—which is, of course, what a PEO does—cuts that cost by two-fifths, according to Small Business Administration figures.

Nor is it only the small enterprises that can cut their labor costs substantially by outsourcing employee relations. A 1997 McKinsey & Co. study concluded that a global Fortune 500 firm—in other words, a very big company indeed—could cut its labor costs by 25 to 33 percent by having its employee relations managed by an outside firm. This study apparently led to the foundation of Exult a year later.

The outsourcing of employees and employee relations is an international trend. Although employment laws and regulations vary widely from country to country, the costs they impose on businesses are high everywhere in the developed world. Adecco's biggest market, for instance, is France (the United States is number two); and Adecco is growing 40 percent a year in Japan. Exult opened a big employee-management center in Scotland in 2000 and has employee-management offices in London and Geneva as well.

Even more onerous than the costs are the enormous demands that regulations place on management time and attention. In the twenty years between 1980 and 2000, the number of U.S. laws and regulations regarding employment policies and practices grew by 60 percent, from thirty-eight to sixty. All of these require reports, and all threaten fines and punishment for noncompliance, even if unintentional. According, again, to the Small Business Administration, the owner of a small or even a midsize business spends up to a full quarter of his or her time on employment-related paperwork. And then there is the constant—and constantly growing—threat of employment-related lawsuits. Between 1991 and 2000, the number of sexual-harassment cases filed with the Equal Employment Opportunity Commission more than doubled, from 6,883 a year to 15,889. And for every case filed, up to ten or more were being settled in-house—each requiring many hours of investigation and hearings, and substantial legal fees as well.

No wonder that employers (and especially the smaller ones, which constitute the overwhelming majority) complain bitterly that they have no time to work on product and service, on customers and markets, on quality and distribution—they have no time to work, that is, on *results*. They instead work on problems, that is, on employee regulations. They no longer chant the old mantra "People are our greatest asset." They now say instead, "People are our greatest liability." What underlies both the success of the temp companies and the emergence of the PEOs is that they *enable management to focus on the business.*

This argument, by the way, can also explain the success of the maquiladoras, the manufacturing plants on the Mexican side of the U.S. border (and increasingly in the interior of Mexico as well) that assemble parts made in the United States, the Far East, or Mexico into finished products for the U.S. market. In fact, I would argue that avoiding onerous paperwork is a stronger incentive for the manufacturing companies than the often questionable labor savings. The Mexican firm that is the maquiladora's landlord acts as the "coemployer," handling all employee regulations and employee activities (which are as complicated in Mexico as they are in the United States), thus freeing the U.S. or Japanese owner of the plant to focus on the business.

There is not the slightest reason to believe that the costs

or the demands of employment rules and regulations will go down in any developed country. On the contrary. No matter how badly needed a patient's bill of rights may be in the United States, it will undoubtedly create another layer of agencies with which an employer has to deal: another set of reports and paperwork; another avalanche of complaints, disputes, and lawsuits.

The Splintered Organization

Beyond the desire to avoid the costs and distractions of regulations, there is another major reason for both the rise of the temps and the emergence of the PEOs: the nature of knowledge work and, most particularly, the extraordinary specialization of knowledge workers. Most large, knowledge-based organizations have lots of different types of specialized workers; managing them all effectively is a big challenge for the organization. Temp agencies and PEOs can help solve that problem.

Not so long ago, even in the 1950s, as many as 90 percent of the workforce were "nonexempt"—subordinates who did as they were told. The "exempt" were supervisors who did the telling. Most nonexempt employees were blue-collar workers who had few skills and little education. They typically did repetitive tasks on the plant floor or in the office. Today less than a fifth of the workforce is blue collar. Knowledge workers (two-fifths of the workforce) may have a supervisor, but they are not "subordinates."

They are "associates." Within their area of knowledge they are supposed to do the telling. But, above all, knowledge workers are not homogeneous. Knowledge is effective only if specialized. This is particularly true of the fastest-growing group of knowledge workers—the fastest-growing group in the workforce altogether—knowledge technologists such as computer repair people, paralegals, programmers, and many others. And because knowledge work is specialized, it is deeply splintered even in large organizations.

The best example is the hospital—altogether the most complex human organization ever devised, but also, in the last thirty or forty years, the fastest-growing one in all developed countries. A fair-size community hospital of 275 or 300 beds will have around three thousand people working for it. Close to half of them will be knowledge workers of one kind or another. Two of these groups—nurses and specialists in the business departments—are fairly large, numbering several hundred people each. But there are around thirty "paramedic specialties": the physical therapists and the people in the clinical lab; the psychiatric caseworkers; the oncological technicians; the two dozen people who prepare patients for surgery; the people in the sleep clinic; the ultrasound technicians; the cardiac-clinic specialists, and many, many more.

Each of these specialties has its own rules and regulations, its own education, its own requirements, its own accreditation. Yet each, in any given hospital, consists of only a handful of people—there may be no more than seven or eight dietitians, for instance, in the 275-bed hospital. Each group, however, expects and requires special treatment. Each expects—and needs—someone higher up who understands what it is doing, what equipment it needs, what its relationship should be to doctors, nurses, the business office. Also, within the individual hospital there are no career-advancement opportunities for any of them; not one of them wants to be the hospital's administrator or has any chance of getting the job.

Few businesses currently have as many specialists as the hospital does. But they're getting there. A department store chain I know of now counts fifteen or sixteen distinct knowledge specialties, most of them employing only a handful each in any one store. In financial services, too, there is increasing specialization and increasing need, apparently, for concentration on one speciality. The person who selects the mutual funds the firm should offer its clients does not sell those mutual funds nor does she service them. And increasingly there are fewer and fewer career opportunities for the individual knowledge specialist within the organization. The experts who select the mutual funds to be offered to retail customers are not going to become mutual-fund salespeople. But they are also not particularly interested in becoming a manager beyond running a small group—a handful of fellow specialists at most.

The American hospital has largely tackled this problem of specialization by piecemeal outsourcing. In many hospitals (perhaps a majority by now) each of the several knowledge specialties is managed by a different outsourcer. Blood transfusion, for instance, is run by a firm that specializes in blood transfusions and manages the transfusion departments of a fairly large number of separate hospitals. Like a PEO, it is the coemployer of the transfusion people. Within the chain the individual transfusion specialists also have career opportunities. If they perform well, they can become managers of the transfusion department at a bigger and better-paying hospital or supervisors of several transfusion units in the chain.

Both the large temp company and the PEO do across the board what in the hospital is done piecemeal. Each of their clients, even the biggest, lacks the critical mass effectively to manage, place, and satisfy the highly specialized knowledge person. And this is what the PEO and the temp agency can provide.

Thus both the temp agency and the PEOs are performing a vital function for the employee as well as for the employer. This explains why the PEOs can claim, and apparently document, that the people whose coemployer it has become report higher satisfaction—in contradiction to everything human-relations theory would have predicted. The metallurgist in the medium-size chemical firm may be well paid and have an interesting job. But the firm needs and employs only a handful of metallurgists. No one in upper management understands what the metallurgist is doing, should be doing, could be doing. There is no opportunity, except a remote one, of becoming an executive, and in any event that would mean giving up what the metallurgist has spent years learning how to do and loves. The well-run temp firm can and does place the metallurgist where he can make the maximum contribution. And it can—and does—place the successful metallurgist in increasingly better and better-paid jobs. And in a PEO full-service contract (and many PEOs won't accept any other), it is expressly provided that the PEO has the duty and the right to place the people whose coemployer it is in the job and in the company where they best fit and belong. How to balance these responsibilities to employing client and employee is probably the PEO's most important job.

Companies Don't Get It

HR policies still assume that most if not all the people who work for a company are employees of that company. But as we have seen, that is not true. Some are temps and others are employees of the outsourcers who manage (say) the company's computer systems or call centers. Still others are older part-time workers who have taken early retirement but still work on specific assignments. With all this splintering, no one is left to view the organization in its entirety. HR organizations and PEOs concern themselves only with the people who are legal employees. Temp agencies claim to be selling productivity—in other words, to be doing the organization's oversight job for them—but it's hard to see how they can deliver. The productivity of the people they supply to a customer depends on placing them, managing them, motivating them. The temp agency has no control over any of these areas. Nor does the PEO.

This lack of oversight is a real problem. Every organization in existence needs employee management that views all the people on whose productivity and performance the organization depends as its responsibility—whether they're temps or part-timers, whether they're employees of the organization itself or of its outsourcers, suppliers, and distributors.

There are signs that we are moving in that direction. A European multinational consumer-goods maker is about to split off its large and highly regarded employee-management function into a separate corporation that will act as the PEO for the parent company throughout the world. But it would also manage the relationships with, and the utilization of, the people who work for the multinational and are not legally its employees. Eventually this in-house PEO will offer itself as the coemployer for the employees of the multinational's suppliers and distributors and for its more than two hundred joint ventures and alliances. And Sony, the Japanese consumer-electronics giant, is experimenting with a plan under which an applicant for a permanent job in one of its major plants must first work for ten months as an Adecco temp. During this time, however, Sony would be the trial employee's personnel manager even though Adecco would be the legal employer.

The Key to Competitive Advantage

Actually it is more important today for organizations to pay close attention to the health and well-being of all their workers than it was fifty years ago. A knowledge-based workforce is qualitatively different from a less skilled workforce. True, knowledge workers are a minority of the total workforce—and are unlikely ever to be more than that. But they are fast becoming the largest single group. And they have already become the major creator of wealth. Increasingly the success, indeed the survival, of every business will depend on the performance of its knowledge workforce. And since it is impossible, according to the laws of statistics, for any but the smallest organization to have "better people," the only way an organization in a knowledge-based economy and society can excel is through getting more out of the same kind of people; that is, through managing its knowledge workers for greater productivity. It is, to repeat an old saying, "to make ordinary people do extraordinary things."

What made the traditional workforce productive was the system—whether it was Frederick Winslow Taylor's "one best way," Henry Ford's assembly line, or Ed Deming's Total Quality Management. The system embodies the knowledge. The system is productive because it enables individual workers to perform without much knowledge or skill. In fact, on the assembly line (but also in Deming's Total Quality Management), greater skill on the part of an

124

individual worker is a threat to coworkers and to the entire system. In a knowledge-based organization, however, it is the individual worker's productivity that makes the system productive. In a traditional workforce the worker serves the system; in a knowledge workforce the system must serve the worker.

There are enough knowledge-based organizations around to show what that means. What makes a university a great university is that it attracts and (above all) develops outstanding teachers and scholars and makes it possible for them to do outstanding teaching and research. The same is true of an opera house. The knowledge-based institution that most nearly resembles a knowledge-based business is the symphony orchestra, in which some thirty different instruments play the same score together as a team. A great orchestra is not composed of great instrumentalists but of adequate ones who produce at their peak. When a new conductor is hired to turn around an orchestra that has suffered years of drifting and neglect, he cannot, as a rule, fire any but a few of the sloppiest or most superannuated players. He also cannot as a rule hire many new orchestra members. He has to make productive what he has inherited. The successful ones do this by working closely with individual members and individual sections. Their "employee relations" are a given and they're nearly unchangeable. Their "people relations" make the difference.

It would be difficult to overstate the importance of focusing on knowledge workers' productivity. For the critical feature of a knowledge workforce is that knowledge workers are not "labor," they are capital. And what is decisive in the performance of capital is not what capital costs. It is not how much capital is being invested—or else the Soviet Union would easily have been the world's foremost economy. What's critical is the *productivity of capital*. What brought about the Soviet Union's economic collapse was that the capital productivity of its investments was so incredibly low—in many cases less than a third that of capital investment in a market economy and sometimes actually negative (as in the case of the huge investments in farming during the Brezhnev years). The reason was simple—no one paid any attention to the productivity of capital, no one had that as their job, no one got rewarded for it.

Private industry in the market economies teaches the same lesson. In new industries, leadership can be obtained—and maintained—by innovation. In an established industry, however, what differentiates the leading company is almost always outstanding productivity of capital. In the early part of the twentieth century, General Electric, for instance, competed through innovations in technology and products with its long-term rival Westinghouse, or with the Europeans such as Siemens. But in the early 1920s, after the era of rapid technology innovation in electromechanics had come to an end, GE concentrated on the productivity of capital to give it decisive leadership, and it has maintained this lead ever since. Similarly, Sears

Roebuck's glory days—from the late 1920s through the 1960s—were not based on merchandise or pricing. Its rivals, such as Montgomery Ward, did just as well in both areas. Sears's leadership was based on getting about twice the work out of a dollar that other American retailers did. Knowledge-based businesses need to be similarly focused on the productivity of their capital, that is, of the knowledge worker.

Free Managers—to Manage People

Temps and especially PEOs free up managers to focus on the business rather than on employment-related rules, regulations, and paperwork. To spend up to one-quarter of one's time on employment-related paperwork is indeed a waste of precious, expensive, scarce resources. It is boring. It demeans and corrupts, and the only thing it can possibly teach is greater skill in cheating.

Companies thus have ample reason to try to do away with the routine chores of employee relations—whether by systematizing employee management in-house, or by outsourcing it to temps or to a PEO. But they need to be careful that they don't damage or destroy people relations in the process. Indeed, the main benefit of decreasing paperwork may be to gain a little more time for people relations. Executives will have to learn what the effective department head in the university or the successful conductor of the symphony orchestra has long known: the key to greatness is to look for the potential of people and to spend time developing it. To build an outstanding university department requires spending time with the promising young postdocs and assistant professors until they excel in their work. To build a world-class orchestra requires rehearsing the same passage in a symphony again and again until the first clarinet plays it the way the conductor hears it. And this is also what makes a research director successful in an industry lab. The one way to achieve leadership in the knowledge-based business is similarly to spend time with the promising knowledge professionals: to get to know them and to be known by them; to mentor them and to listen to them; to challenge them and to encourage them. These people may no longer legally be the organization's employees. But they will still be the organization's resource and capital and the key to its performance. Employee relations can—and indeed should—be systematized; and that means that they can—perhaps should—become impersonal. But that should make people relations all the more important. If employee relations are being outsourced, executives need to work closely with their counterparts in the outsourcer on the professional development, the motivation, the satisfaction, and the productivity of the knowledge people on whose performance their own performance and results depend—maybe the main (though unspoken) lesson of the BP Amoco story related earlier.

. . .

Two hundred and fifty years ago, in what we now call the Industrial Revolution, the permanent large organization emerged. The cotton mill and the railroad were the first ones. But while unprecedented, they were still based on manual labor, as was all earlier work. Manual labor—whether it was farming, manufacturing, clearing checks by hand, or entering life-insurance claims into a ledger—was still the work of the great majority as late as fifty or sixty years ago, even in the most highly developed economies. The emergence of knowledge work and of the knowledge worker—let alone their emergence as the "capital" of a knowledge-based society and knowledge-based economy—is thus as profound a change as was the Industrial Revolution 250 years ago, perhaps an even greater one. It will require more than a few new programs and a few new practices, however helpful they are. It will require new measurements, new values, new goals, and new policies. It will predictably take a good many years before we have worked these out. However, there are enough successful knowledge-based organizations around to tell us what the basic assumption has to be for managing employees in a knowledge-based organization. It has to be that employees may indeed be our greatest liabilities, but people are our greatest opportunity.

(2002)

9

Financial Services: Innovate or Die

The rebirth in the past forty years of London's City as a world financial center is as impressive a success story as is Silicon Valley. The City today is not nearly as powerful or as important as it was in the hundred years between Waterloo and the First World War. Still, today's City, through its interbank market, is the banking system's "central banker" worldwide. It is the world's largest foreign exchange market. The money for medium-term financing (e.g., "bridge loans" or the financing of mergers and acquisitions) may be raised in America, but more often than not the structure of these complicated deals is being worked out in London. Even in long-term financing such as underwriting, the City is outranked only by New York.

Yet in 1960, no one would have expected the City's

resurgence. After fifty years of steady decline it was then considered almost irrelevant even by many people in the City itself.

To some extent the City's turnaround was made possible by two American events, both occurring during the Kennedy administration. At the time of the Cuban missile crisis, the Russian State Bank, afraid of having its American accounts frozen, shifted its foreign reserves into London. But the Russians wanted to keep their money in dollars. And thus the Eurodollar was born—a transnational currency denominated in dollars but domiciled in London. Shortly thereafter the American administration— foolishly—put a punitive tax on payments of interest to foreigners, thus destroying in one fell swoop the flourishing New York foreign-bond market. It fled, giving birth to the Eurobond—again denominated mostly in dollars but domiciled and controlled in London.

These American events only created an opportunity. London bankers—and especially S. G. Warburg—seized it. Indeed S. G. Warburg, a firm started only in the 1930s by two German refugees, had, even earlier, in 1959, brought an entrepreneurial form of banking to London when it began to finance acquisitions. Until then this kind of entrepreneurial finance had for seventy-five years been an American speciality (i.e., since J. P. Morgan in the 1880s).

But the key factor in the City's rebirth as a financial center was its recovering its nineteenth-century position as the headquarters for financial institutions from all over the world. The nineteenth-century City was the creation of an earlier immigrant from Germany, Nathan Rothschild. After the Napoleonic wars, he invented the capital market by financing the governments of Europe and of newly independent Latin America through bonds underwritten in London, placed in London, and traded on the London Stock Exchange. He was soon followed by a host of other immigrants—Schroder (Germany); Hambros (Norway); Lazard (France); Morgan (America)—to name but a few.

These newcomers typically founded English firms and many became British themselves. But together with some of the older English-born "merchant bankers" (such as Baring Brothers, a bank founded by the sons of a German emigrant in 1770), they created a truly global financial center.

What attracted these immigrants was not just that England was the nineteenth-century's foremost trading country. It was that London soon became the world's foremost financial-knowledge center (as Walter Bagehot first pointed out in his 1873 book, *Lombard Street*). This, too, was largely Nathan Rothschild's invention and legacy. The five Rothschild brothers—each stationed in a different European financial capital, but all five acting as one firm with Nathan as the chief executive—were an early "intranet," with their famous carrier pigeons a pre-electronic "e-mail." To this day, despite all the vicissitudes of this century, the City has remained the sole worldwide knowledge center for business, finance, and economic affairs. And it is the City as transnational knowledge center that, in the

1960s and 1970s, again attracted "financial immigrants" to London from all over the world. Legally, these London establishments are wholly owned subsidiaries or branches of an American, Swiss, Dutch, or German parent. But in economic reality these subsidiaries tend to be separate and largely autonomous, that is "headquarters." It is a common saying on Wall Street that the New York office, whether of Goldman Sachs or of Citibank, is primarily concerned with the firm's domestic business. The firm's international business is largely directed out of London.

A Wider Transformation

The rebirth of the City was, however, only the first chapter in the success story of financial services in the past forty years. That this is a new industry is largely concealed by the fact that many of its big players bear old, and often nineteenth-century, names. But the Goldman Sachs of 1999 is a very different business from the Goldman Sachs of 1899, of 1929, or even of 1959—and so are J. P. Morgan, Merrill Lynch, First Boston, Citibank, GE Capital, or any of the other big firms, whether American or European. Even in 1950 all these were still domestic institutions.

It may be indicative that when I first came to the United States from England in the mid-1930s, only two of the top New York banks—Manufacturers and Guaranty Trust, both long gone through mergers—had an executive in charge of foreign business, and neither ever made full vice president. The only things these two "assistant VPs international" then did were to issue letters of credit to American exporters and to provide importers with foreign currency. Anything beyond that was sent to a "correspondent bank" in the foreign country.

Even the few financial firms that then had establishments outside their home country (as both Deutsche Bank and what is now Citibank had in South America) used these "branches" primarily to serve their own domestic clients. "Our first job," the head of one of the most prosperous South American branches of what is now Citibank said to me in the early 1950s, "is to be to American business what American Express is to the American tourist."

But today all these firms have become global and operate "transnationally." They are everywhere, in all the main business capitals. Every main establishment is a headquarters in its own right. Its mission now is no longer to serve the domestic customers of its parent. It is to become a major player in both the domestic and the international business of the country in which it is located.

Equally radical is the change in the business itself. These financial services institutions are neither commercial bankers, nor investment bankers, nor merchant bankers, nor stockbrokers—the typical financial businesses of 1950. Some still offer the traditional services—but few try to push them. In fact, today's main financial services products barely existed at an earlier time. Some examples: managing and financing mergers, acquisitions, and divestitures, both friendly and hostile; financing equipment

leasing worldwide; financing the global expansion of manufacturing and commercial companies. And there was
nothing remotely like the enormous business in currencies
now generated by world trade and investment.

While the new financial services industry began with the
rebirth of London's City in the early 1960s, it soon became
worldwide after 1970. But despite its success—indeed
largely because of it—the industry will have to reinvent itself if it is to continue to prosper in the twenty-first century.
The products that fueled its growth—beginning with the
Eurodollar and Eurobond, that is with the rebirth of
London's City—can no longer sustain it. Forty years ago
they were innovations. Now they have become "commodities," which means they have become increasingly low-
profit, if not unprofitable. And for each deal there seems
to be many bidders. The one who snares the deal may
make lots of money despite his heavy expenses. But others
have only the expenses. So more and more of the income
of the top firms—whether owned by Americans, Germans,
Dutch, or Swiss—no longer comes from fees that clients
pay for services. It comes from trading for the firm's own
account—in stocks and bonds, in derivatives, currencies,
and commodities.

Every financial services firm has to do some trading
for its own account. It is a routine part of managing the
firm's own finances and is aimed at minimizing risk, e.g.,
by bridging gaps between the maturity dates of what the
firm owes and what is being owed. Beyond this, a certain
amount of trading for the firm's own account can and

should be profitable with minimal risk; it exploits the firm's knowledge of the markets. But when trading for a firm's own account becomes the major activity, it ceases to be "trading" and has become "gambling." And no matter how clever the gambler, the laws of probability guarantee that he will eventually lose all he has gained, and then a good deal more.

This is already happening to the leading financial services firms. Almost every big firm has by now reported substantial "trading losses." In several cases the losses have been so heavy as to kill the firm. One example is Barings, the world's oldest and most respected London private bank; what is left of it is now owned by a Dutch financial group. Similar trading losses forced New York's Bankers Trust—not so long ago one of the most respected international banks—to sell itself to Germany's Deutsche Bank. Several Japanese financial giants survived their trading losses (e.g., Sumitomo speculating in copper) only because Japan Inc. came to their rescue. But even Japan Inc. could not save Yamaichi, one of the largest Tokyo stockbrokers, from losses it incurred by trading in property for its own account.

In every single one of these trading losses, the firm's top management has claimed that it knew nothing of the gambles, and that the gambling trader violated the firm's rules. But in the first place there is a limit to coincidences. Such widespread breakdowns cannot be blamed on "exceptions." They denote systems failure. But also, in every single one of these "scandals," top management seems carefully to have looked the other way as long as trading produced profits (or at least pretended to produce them). Until the losses had become so big that they could no longer be hidden, the gambling trader was a hero and showered with money.

No industry can survive, let alone prosper, unless it is paid for services rendered to others, that is, to outside clients and customers. But the customers of the financial firms that trade for their own account are other financial firms trading for their own account. And this is a "zero-sum game" with one firm's gains being another firm's losses—and nothing left over to pay either's expenses.

There is still one area for genuine growth in present financial services: Japan. Its financial system is still largely pre-1950 and thoroughly antiquated. Japan is slowly allowing foreigners in to provide modern financial services; and whenever they have been let in, the foreigners—primarily Americans, but also Germans, French, and British—have fast become successful and leaders. They are, for instance, the key players in Tokyo's foreign exchange market. Similarly, foreign firms increasingly handle the non-Japanese investments of Japanese pension funds and insurance companies—and they may soon be allowed to become Japanese-pension-fund managers themselves. And an American firm, Merrill Lynch, can now serve both retail and institutional investors in Japan, thanks to its purchase of Yamaichi.

But Japan could be the "last hurrah" of the financial services industry in its present form. In volume, demand for the products of today's industry may grow in the next few years as European and Asian industries speed up their restructuring—still far behind America. But the industry's profitability is unlikely to recover. The industry's traditional products and services have been around so long that there is an oversupply of people and firms proficient in them. There is thus less and less true differentiation between what different financial services firms can offer. The customers know it and are increasingly shopping around for the best deal.

Time for Innovations

The reason that the financial services industry is in trouble is quite simple. The dominant financial services institutions have not made a single major innovation in thirty years.

The two decades between 1950 and 1970 brought one innovation after the other. The Eurodollar and the Eurobond were just two of them. There was the institutional investor—started off by the creation of the first modern pension fund, the General Motors fund in 1950, which set off a veritable boom in corporate pension funds but also turned the then still marginal mutual fund into a central financial institution. Within a few years this led to the foundation of the first firm specifically designed to service new institutional investors: Donaldson, Lufkin and Jenrette, in New York. At roughly the same time, Felix Rohatyn in New York (later American ambassador to France) invented the new role of the private banker as initiator and manager of acquisitions, especially of hostile ones.

The 1960s saw also the invention of the credit card— now ubiquitous and becoming "legal tender," especially in the developed countries. It is largely the credit card that has enabled commercial banks to survive even though much of their traditional business of commercial loans has been siphoned off by the new financial services institutions. The remaining innovations were both made by Walter Wriston (born 1919) shortly after he became head of Citibank in 1967. He almost immediately changed his company from being an American bank with foreign branches into a global bank with multiple headquarters. And his insight, a few years later, that "banking is not about money; it is about information," created what I would call the "theory of the business" for the financial services industry.

Since then, thirty years ago, the only innovations have been any number of allegedly "scientific" derivatives. But these financial instruments are not designed to provide a service to customers. They are designed to make the trader's speculations more profitable and at the same time less risky—surely a violation of the basic laws of risk and unlikely to work. In fact, they are unlikely to work better than the inveterate gambler's equally "scientific" systems for beating the odds at Monte Carlo or Las Vegas—as a good many traders have already found out. Otherwise, however, there have only been minor improvements—

doing a little better what was already done quite well. As a result, the industry's products have become commodities and increasingly both less profitable and more expensive to sell.

This is, of course, what both economic theory and experience could have predicted. In fact, the trajectory of the financial services industry is a textbook example of the two classic innovation theories, that of the French economist J. B. Say in his 1803 book, *Traité de l'économie politique* (Treatise on Political Economy), and of the Austro-American Joseph Schumpeter in his 1912 book, *Theorie der Wirtschaftlichen Entwicklung* (Theory of Economic Development).

Say explained, at the outset of the Industrial Revolution, why there could not be too many cotton mills using the new inventions of the spinning jenny and steam engine, and all of them hugely profitable. He showed that such inventions in the beginning create their own, insatiable demand, and thus create in their early stages higher profitability for all, the more of them there are. Schumpeter, a little over a century later, then showed that this stage cannot last long for the simple reason that the high "innovator's profit" soon attracts too many imitators. The industry then changes from one making and selling highly profitable products and services to one making and selling profitless commodities, even if demand still remains strong.

There are now only three possible roads the financial services industry can take. The easiest, and usually the most heavily traveled, is to keep on doing what worked in the past. Going down this road means, however, steady decline. The industry may survive—there are still plenty of cotton mills, after all. But no matter how hard it works, it will keep on going downhill.

The second road is for the industry to be replaced by innovating outsiders and newcomers—Schumpeter's "creative destruction." This is basically what happened to the old London "City" thirty-five years ago. Except for Rothschild and Schroder, not one of the leading City firms of 1950–60 is still in English hands, not even Warburg. All have become wholly owned subsidiaries of foreign firms: American, Dutch, Swiss, German, French.

For today's financial services industry, the first road is surely not open. There is far too much change going on in the world—social, economic, technological, political—for a major but ailing industry to be left alone. There is far too much money to be made by taking pieces of lucrative business away from the struggling giants, especially those that are preoccupied with trading to the neglect of their legitimate businesses. And with Web sites and e-commerce, it is easy for outsiders to enter the industry if they have something new and truly different to offer.

The second road—to be replaced, and probably fairly rapidly, by outsider innovators—remains a possibility for today's firms. But there is also a third and final road—to become innovators themselves and their own "creative destroyers."

There is no lack of opportunities for new and highly profitable financial services. Indeed the biggest—and probably most profitable—opportunity does not require innovation at all. It requires only hard work. It lies in demographics; that is, in serving the new and different financial needs of the rapidly growing affluent and aging middle class in developed and emerging countries. These people are not "rich" and are thus not attractive customers for the traditional financial firms. But while their individual purchases are relatively modest—rarely more than $30,000–$50,000 a year per family—the sums they collectively pour into investments dwarf by several orders of magnitude everything all the world's "superrich" together have available, including oil sheikhs, Indonesian rajas, and software billionaires.

This market was discovered thirty years ago by Edward Jones, a then minuscule and totally obscure provincial brokerage firm in St. Louis, Missouri. When he discovered this market, Edward Jones decided to drop all other business and exclusively serve the individual, middle-class investor—small-business owners, middle managers, successful professionals, and so on; and to sell nothing not appropriate to this group. It is now a major national firm and has been highly profitable all along. And that this market is not confined to America, Edward Jones proved when, a few years ago, it went into England and opened offices in small towns around London. Totally unknown, and with an approach to business, to investments, and to customers that was—and still is—new, it found an immediate response.

The Jones type of customer constitutes the fastest-growing population group in every developed and emerging country. In addition to North America, this includes all of Europe, the most populous countries of Latin America, Japan, and South Korea, but also the metropolitan areas of mainland China—close to half of the human population.

This market might become the twenty-first century's successor to the world's first financial "mass market": life insurance. By providing financial protection against the major eighteenth- and nineteenth-century risk of dying too soon, life insurance became the biggest financial industry of that century, growing profitably worldwide for more than 150 years, i.e., until 1914. Providing financial protection against the new risk of not dying soon enough may well become the next century's major and most profitable financial industry.

Here is another example—but one where the business has yet to be built: being the "outsourcing" and financial manager for medium-size businesses. Except in Japan and South Korea, medium-size firms dominate all developed economies—but also the emerging economies, whether in Latin America or in Taiwan. The eighty thousand *Mittelstand* (i.e., medium-size) businesses are the backbone of Germany's economy. And similar businesses are also the backbone of the American, French, Dutch, Italian, Brazilian, and Argentinean economies.

In terms of products, technology, marketing, and customer service, the medium-size businesses usually have the needed critical mass. But in financial management many—perhaps most—do not have the size to support the competence they need. Typically, for instance, they operate with a woefully low productivity of capital and have either too little or too much cash. An increasing number already outsource their data processing and information systems; their housekeeping; their routine personnel management; and even a good deal of research and product development. How long will it be before they are ready to outsource the management of the money in their business?

The tools for doing this work are fully developed, e.g., EVA (economic value analysis), or cash-flow forecast and cash-flow management. The financial management needs of these businesses are predictable. And worldwide they fall into a small number of categories, well-known to any experienced commercial banker. The rewards for building a firm providing these medium-size businesses with financial management might be enormous—not only from fees but also through substantial profits from "securitizing" the financial needs of the clients, i.e., converting them into investment products that should be particularly attractive to the aging middle-class "retail" investor.

A final example of a potential opportunity for new financial services: financial instruments that protect a business against catastrophic foreign-exchange losses by converting currency risks into an ordinary cost of doing business, with an affordable and fixed premium, maybe no more than 3–5 percent of a firm's currency exposure. Again most of the knowledge for such an instrument—half insurance, half investment—is largely available: the actuarial concepts to determine needed sample size and risk mix; the knowledge of risk management; the economic knowledge and data to identify endangered currencies, and so on.

The need is desperate—again, mostly among the world's huge numbers of middle-size businesses that suddenly find themselves exposed to a chaotic global economy. No business, except an exceptional very big one, can protect itself against this risk by itself. Only aggregation, which subjects the risks to probability, could do so. And again, such a financial services firm would also be able to "securitize" its portfolio and thereby create attractive investments for the new financial retail market.

These are just examples and—except for the already existing and already served retail market of the affluent aging—still hypothetical ones. If they were developed, however, they might have tremendous impact on existing financial services institutions. Outsourcing financial management of middle-size companies might, for instance, wipe out practically overnight a good deal of the most profitable business of such financial services companies as GE Capital. Making catastrophic currency risk insurable might similarly make obsolete most of the foreign-exchange business of existing institutions, let alone their frantic currency trading and speculation in derivatives.

Financial Services: Innovate or Die

After twenty-five years of pooh-poohing the middle-class investment market, some of the traditional American financial services institutions have lately come to accept its existence and importance. Merrill Lynch, for instance, is aggressively moving into it. Whether this will work still remains to be seen. It is quite likely that—as in many other retail businesses—success in this market demands exclusive concentration on it; and Merrill Lynch is trying to combine being the financial services provider for this highly distinctive market with offering a host of other, and mostly very traditional, financial services.

But outside of this market—which is, after all, now thirty years old—there are no signs that any of the large global financial services firms are even experimenting with these potential new businesses or with anything else that might be an innovation. These new businesses require long years of patient, conscientious hard work—and that may not fit the trader's mentality that now seems to rule the big and dominant financial services firms. Yet it is highly probable—indeed almost predictable—that somebody, somewhere, is already working on these or similar new financial services, which, when introduced, will replace, or render unprofitable, today's financial services.

It may not be too late for the existing big financial services firms to become innovators again. But it is surely very late.

(1999)

10

Moving Beyond Capitalism?

This interview was conducted by Nathan Gardels, editor of *New Perspectives Quarterly*, in the author's office in Claremont, California. It was based on the author's specifying the topics and the interviewer's questions. The author himself edited the interviewer's draft into the final text. The interview appeared in *New Perspectives Quarterly* in the spring 1998 issue.

Of late, some of capitalism's biggest boosters, people such as yourself and the financier George Soros, have become its biggest critics.

What is your critique?

I am for the free market. Even though it doesn't work too well, nothing else works at all. But I have serious reservations about capitalism as a system because it idolizes economics as the be-all and end-all of life. It is one-dimensional.

For example, I have often advised managers that a 20–1 salary ratio is the limit beyond which they cannot go if they don't want resentment and falling morale to hit their companies. I worried back in the 1930s that the great inequality generated by the Industrial Revolution would result in so much despair that something like fascism would take hold. Unfortunately, I was right.

Today, I believe it is socially and morally unforgivable when managers reap huge profits for themselves but fire workers. As societies, we will pay a heavy price for the contempt this generates among the middle managers and workers.

In short, whole dimensions of what it means to be a human being and treated as one are not incorporated into the economic calculus of capitalism. For such a myopic system to dominate other aspects of life is not good for any society.

With regard to the market, there are several serious problems with the theory itself.

First of all, the theory assumes there is one homogeneous market. In reality, there are three overlapping markets that, by and large, don't interchange: an international market in money and information, national markets, and local markets.

Most of what passes for transnational economic money, of course, is only virtual money.

The London interbank market each day has a greater volume of activity in dollar terms than the whole world would need for a year to finance all economic transactions.

This is functionless money. It cannot possibly earn any return since it serves no function. It has no purchasing power. It is, therefore, totally speculative and prone to panics as it rushes here and there to earn that last 64th of 1 percent.

Then, there is a large national economy which is not exposed to international commerce. Some 24 percent of U.S. economic activity is exposed to trade. In Japan, it is only 8 percent.

Then there is the local economy. The hospital near my home has very high-quality care and is very competitive. But it does not compete with any hospital forty miles away in Los Angeles. The effective market area for hospitals in the U.S. is about ten miles because, for some obscure reason no economist would be able to figure out, people like to be close to their sick mothers.

Also, what drives markets has changed. The economic center of gravity shifted sometime during this century. In the nineteenth century, with steel and steam, supply generated demand. Since the Great Depression, however, the tables have turned: In traditional products, from home construction to cars, demand must come before supply— although this is not yet true today of information and electronics, which stimulate demand.

Beyond this definition of markets, the truly profound

issue is that market theory is based on an assumption of equilibrium and thus cannot accommodate change, let alone innovation.

Rather, the real pattern of economic activity, as Joseph Schumpeter recognized as long ago as 1911, is "a moving disequilibrium" caused by the process of creative destruction as new markets with new products and new demand are made at the expense of old ones.

Market outcomes cannot, therefore, be explained in terms of what the theory would have predicted. The market is in fact not a predictable system, but inherently unstable. And if it is not predictable, you cannot base your behavior on it. That is a pretty serious limitation for a theory of human behavior.

All we can say is that, in the end, any long-term equilibrium is the result of a lot of short-term adaptations to market signals.

This, finally, is the strength of the market: It is a disciplinarian for the short term. By providing feedback through prices, it discourages you from squandering time and resources going off in all directions like King Arthur's knights.

The old idea was that if you rode on long enough you would run into something. The market tells you that if you don't run into something in five weeks, you better change course or do something else.

Beyond the short term, the market is useless. You know, I have sat in on more than my share of research planning for large companies. Fundamentally, this activity is an act of faith. When the chief financial officer asks, as he always does, "What will be the return?" on this or that project, the only answer is "We will know in ten years."

Years ago you wrote about pension fund ownership of the American economy, calling it "capitalism sans capitalists" where workers' retirement funds own the means of production.

Today, this dispersion of wealth has gone even further through the explosion of mutual funds—more than 51 percent of Americans own shares of stock.

Have we arrived at mass capitalism or postcapitalism?

Well, to call it postcapitalism is merely to say we don't know what to call it.

You also can't call it economic democracy since there is no organized form of governance associated with this mass ownership.

What is certain is that it is a totally new phenomenon in history.

My gardener, who is not a wealthy man, takes the "money markets" section of the *Wall Street Journal* I put out for him at the back door every week to guide his stock investments.

A friend of mine who works with a regional financial service that has 2 million accounts told me recently that his average investor has gone from putting $10,000 per year to $25,000 per year in his mutual fund.

Perhaps it is becoming true that capitalists don't matter anymore. In earlier periods of the adoration of the rich, there were strongly voiced opinions either that "we need the rich for capital formation" or "the rich are just exploiting us all." One doesn't hear either of these opinions anymore.

J. P. Morgan once mattered to the American economy. At his peak, he had enough liquid capital to finance all capital needs in America for four months.

Adjusting for inflation, J. P. Morgan probably had a little less than a third of what Bill Gates has today. Such wealth possessed by one man has not been seen in the world since the time of the great Khan of China. But Gates's $40 billion could only finance the American economy for less than one day.

Bill Gates is important because of the Microsoft company he built and the software we use. As a rich man, he is totally irrelevant. How he spends or wastes his money will have no impact on the American economy. It is a drop in the bucket.

The wealth that makes the difference in America today is that held by tens of millions of small investors.

Historically, state socialism has failed to produce wealth or efficiently provide social services. Yet capitalism ignores any other dimension of life besides economic exchange. And, as you say, the market is only short-term. How does society, then, manage in the long term?

We now know that we need three sectors, not two. Not just government and business, but what people now call the civil society or third sector in between.

Indeed, I believe that the realistic alternative to the socialist delusion on one hand, and the pure market on the other, combines the dispersed ownership of the economy through pension and mutual funds with a "third" nonprofit sector to cope with community needs from health care to tutoring students.

The idea that some of my Republican friends have that we can do without government is just silly. It is an understandable reaction because of the postwar belief that government could take care of all community needs.

But we have learned that government, like any other tool, is good for some things but not good for others. It is important, for example, for collective defense and for raising the financial means for infrastructure through taxes.

But, just as I am unlikely to do well trying to cut my toenails with a hammer, government is incompetent at fulfilling community needs. Everything a state does, it has to do on a national level. It cannot experiment or adapt to the local conditions of a community.

The state tends to define a problem in a standard way and then monopolizes the solution. But what works in St. Louis usually doesn't work even in Kansas City, let alone New York or Los Angeles.

With its singular profit motive, of course, the market simply has no interest or capacity to cope with social problems.

Though people think of me mainly as a management consultant for business, I have spent much of my time for fifty years consulting for nonprofit organizations. Fifteen years ago, there were only three hundred thousand tax-exempt nonprofit groups registered with the IRS, including such well-known groups as the American Heart Association and the American Lung Association. Now there are over 1 million.

I also helped set up a foundation for nonprofit management, run by the former national executive of the Girl Scouts. The idea was simple: These organizations are not so much mismanaged as unmanaged. Without market discipline, they need a focused mission and a results orientation as their bottom line.

One of the problems our foundation has had is the overwhelming demand from countries as diverse as Japan, Brazil, Argentina, and Poland. They all need social sector institutions desperately—from the establishment of nursing associations to battered women's shelters to crop education for peasants in places like Patagonia.

Why is the social sector growing in Japan, where the community has been so strong?

Well, two things are happening. First, the traditional community structure is crumbling. Second, educated women who have worked for a few years, then left work to have children, who then go off to school, are bored.

What kind of social problems does Japan have? When you reach fifty-five years of age in Japan, you are essentially thrown on the dung heap—even though you will probably live thirty years longer. So, the elderly organize clubs, from sports to ikebana flower arranging, to keep themselves occupied.

One of the most successful new social sector groups in Japan engages in that most un-Japanese of activities: "meals on wheels" for the elderly who can't get out.

Young people don't take care of the elderly anymore. Yet, the government fought the establishment of the meals-on-wheels program because it meant they had to admit their old people were not doing so well. Indeed, this is a blot on the Japanese honor. But it is a fact.

There is also a tremendous need among teenagers and school-age children to drive them to and from school, to supervise homework, and tutor those who do not make the top grades.

Nobody outside Japan seems to know that while 20 percent of Japanese students excel, the rest who don't are simply forgotten. The social sector tries to provide for these kids.

There are also conversation and reading classes in English for Japanese women who learned a little in high school or at work and want to maintain it. There are now over 185,000 of these circles, even in small towns.

In Japan now there is even an Alcoholics Anonymous Association. I don't know how big they are so far, but sometimes it seems every salaryman in the country could become a member.

In the U.S., though, the size of the social problems means they just can't be taken care of by voluntary associations, can they?

Perhaps not entirely. But the scope of activities is just tremendous. More than 50 percent of Americans work at least four hours a week in a voluntary association of some sort, in the church or the community.

And the solutions to community problems they come up with are highly creative. I have come over the years to learn a very important lesson: Practical examples of how to solve social problems matter greatly because others will replicate them.

To this end, each year the Drucker Foundation gives a prize to a voluntary association to highlight their example so they can be replicated.

One year, we gave the prize to a very small group run by an immigrant who found a way to bring together the worst, most unproductive welfare mothers and the most seriously disabled children. This led to a situation where the disabled were cared for and, in time, the welfare mothers became qualified to be fully employed and well paid.

There is another project we highlighted by a Lutheran church in St. Louis. In their area, they found that about two-fifths of the homeless, mostly families, need very little to get back on their feet.

The first thing the church did was assess what homeless families needed most. The answer was self-respect.

So the members of the congregation would buy dilapidated houses and find volunteers to refurbish them into comfortable middle-class homes. Then they moved the homeless family in. That by itself changed their outlook on life. Then designated church members would help the family with their bills and in finding work. In the end, about 80 percent of the families in their program went permanently off any kind of assistance.

Then there are organizations such as the Girl Scouts that are reaching new levels of participation. A few years ago they were down to about five hundred thousand volunteers. Today they are up to about nine hundred thousand.

The old volunteer was usually a middle-class housewife bored at home. The new volunteer is more often than not a professional woman who has postponed having children, but likes to be with girls on the weekend after having worked all week in a male environment.

For most of the last twenty-five years, I have worked with the fast-growing Protestant megachurches in the U.S., which I believe are one of the most significant social phenomena in the world today. They teach community activism and encourage people to live their faith by taking action to improve the lives of others.

While the traditional churches may be dying in some ways, in others they are being transformed.

Take the Catholic Church in America. Pope John Paul II has been very careful to place conservative bishops in the American church because it frightens him. It is not so much the theological problems, married priests, and ordained women that bother him, but the enormous upsurge of activity in the dioceses that is lay-driven and not controlled by the bishop.

In one of the larger Midwestern dioceses that I know,

there used to be seven hundred priests; now there are barely more than two hundred and fifty. There are almost no nuns now—but there are twenty-five hundred lay-women. Every parish has a lay administrator who is a woman.

All the priest does is say Mass and dispense the sacraments. Women run the rest of the show entirely as volunteers. That is a long way from the days of the altar girl.

Why does the U.S. have such a large and vital third sector when compared to other countries, including other Western countries?

No other country has anywhere near the scale of activity the U.S. has in the nonprofit sector because, elsewhere essentially, the civil servants of the modern national state destroyed the community sector.

In France it is almost a crime to do anything in the community. The voluntary sector in Victorian England was quite large. It dealt with poverty, with crime, with prostitution, with housing. But in the 20th century the welfare state almost destroyed it.

In Europe the basic struggle was to free the state from the domination of the church, which explains why continental Europe has such an enormous anticlerical tradition.

In the U.S., it was the other way around. When Jonathan Edwards established the doctrine of separation of church and state around 1740, it was in order to free the church from the state. Anticlericalism has never had a place in this country.

Because of this freedom, the U.S. developed a tradition

of religious pluralism and nongovernmental churches. And with pluralism, there was competition among the denominations for members. Out of that competition came a tradition of community involvement which doesn't exist in other countries.

Aside from Jefferson's University of Virginia, all colleges in the U.S. were denominational until Oberlin was established in 1833.

The Asian Crisis

The economic troubles in Asia don't really interest me all that much because what you can fix with money is unlikely to be much of a problem unless you are stupid.

And Asians are not stupid. Fundamentally, the Asian crisis is not economic, but social. Across the entire region, the social tensions are so high that it reminds me of the Europe of my youth that descended into two world wars.

In many ways, we see in Asia the same kind of tensions that arose in Europe as a result of the "great disturbance" of the mass Industrial Revolution and the rapid urbanization that accompanied it. Only Asia's disturbance has taken place at a vastly accelerated pace.

When I first came to know Korea in the 1950s, it was 80 percent rural and practically nobody had more than a high school education because the occupying Japanese hadn't allowed it.

(Only the Christian missionary schools could function

because they couldn't be suppressed by the Japanese, which explains why 30 percent of Koreans are Christians.)

There was no industry because the Japanese didn't allow anyone to have more than a few employees.

Today, Korea is almost 90 percent urban, an industrial powerhouse, and its population is highly educated. All in forty years.

The dislocations of this topsy-turvy development in only four decades have been explosive.

Add to this the unrivaled stupidity of the Korean businessmen who learned nothing from the Japanese next door about how to treat their workers. Japan learned the hard way—through two bloody strikes that almost overturned the government in 1948 and 1954—to treat human beings like human beings. (Nobody seems to know that Japan had had the world's worst history of labor troubles dating back to 1700.)

When foreigners would visit an electronics plant in Korea, if one of the assembly-line women so much as even looked up, she was taken out and beaten for not paying attention to her work.

The autocrats of Korean business not only treated the workers horribly, but kept control of all the money and power in their companies. They treated middle management like black Mississippi schoolteachers in the old days of segregation.

The autocrats then worked hand in hand with the military to keep their power and keep the workers down.

This is finally all changing now with Kim Dae Jung,

but it has left a legacy of deep hatred between Korean business and its workers.

In Malaysia, despite efforts over the years by the government, the tension between the Malays, who are 70 percent of the population, and the Chinese, who are 30 percent, remains high.

Prime Minister Mohamad Mahathir once asked me to advise him on how to keep the Malays in school. So, I visited some villages and found that everything grows there—plantains, bananas, coconuts, apples. And they have pigs and chickens. Nobody has to lift a finger to eat. If they can make enough money for a TV set and a motorbike by working a few hours a year, what more would they want? Why stay in school beyond the third grade?

The Chinese in Malaysia, in contrast, not only stay beyond third grade but go to graduate school in the U.S. They speak English as well as Malay. They know three Chinese dialects.

So, they control things more than Malaysia's leaders want to admit. And they are resented as a result.

It is usually reported that the ethnic Chinese constitute only about 3 percent of the 200 million people of Indonesia, 100 million of whom do not live on Java. This is only true statistically, as the Chinese constitute more than 20 percent of the population in the three major cities, including Jakarta.

In any event, since half a million Chinese were killed in the takeover in the 1960s, they knew they had to stand with the army and its boss, Suharto. So, the Chinese made the money for the Suharto clan and the military and the Muslim population resents it deeply.

Collectively, the "overseas Chinese" have become one of the world's great economic powers. They own businesses wherever they are. They often constitute the professional class wherever they are and are influential with the leadership group. With the exception of Singapore, Taiwan, and Hong Kong—which are all Chinese—they are resented everywhere else.

China itself has had a peasant rebellion every fifty years since 1700. The last one, under Mao, succeeded in 1949.

So, the time is due for another revolt. The problem has always been the same, and it remains today: There are too many unemployed or unemployable peasants with no place to go.

Some estimate that today as many as 200 million peasants constitute a "floating population" that wander around looking for work. And they are not likely to find it. If the Chinese government is serious about shutting down inefficient state industries, another 80 to 100 million people will be on the streets.

Perhaps the history of fascism and war in Europe makes me oversensitive. But I know from personal experience that when social tensions are high, it does not take much more than an accident to set things off.

Therefore, I am afraid for Asia.

On Japan

The leading power in Asia is Japan. But Japan is essentially a European country. Worse, it is a traditional nineteenth-century European country. And that is why it is mired in paralysis today.

Like the Austria of my father's day or France in its heyday, Japan is a country run by a civil service bureaucracy. Politicians don't matter and have always been suspect. If they are incompetent or corrupt, it is to be expected. But if the civil servants turn out to be corrupt and incompetent, it is a terrific shock. Japan is in shock today.

Just as in Japan, the senior civil servant in countries like Germany or France who oversees a certain sector of the economy would usually graduate at about age fifty-five to become a board member of the businesses he was regulating or the head of that sector's trade group at a very fat salary.

Japan is only more organized. The bureaucrat remains loyal to his ministry until the end and defends its turf against all intrusions—even at the cost, in the case of the finance ministry, of sinking the economy. He is then placed by the ministry in a very lucrative "counselorship" in the industry.

The idea that Japanese industry is efficient and competitive is total nonsense. They still have the lowest percent of their economy—about 8 percent and mostly in automobiles and electronics—exposed internationally.

As a consequence, Japan has very little world economy experience. Most of its industry is protected and grotesquely inefficient.

If, for example, Japan were to open its paper industry to imports, the three big Japanese paper companies would be gone in forty-eight hours.

Whenever there has been an opening in the Japanese economy in financial services, Americans and other foreigners have taken over. The foreign exchange business in Japan is completely in the hands of foreign companies.

To be a foreign exchange trader, you need to be at least bilingual because you need to speak English. Not much Japanese is spoken in Geneva.

When a tiny opening in asset management was allowed, 100 percent of the business was taken over by foreign companies within six months. There are few trained asset managers in Japan.

When I look at a Japanese bank today, I see the same bank my father managed in Austria right after World War I. There were four people to do what one could. In 1923, they still didn't believe in typewriters. They had no adding machines.

Though woefully inefficient and overstaffed, the bank was profitable because the many craftsmen of the Austro-Hungarian empire didn't mind paying 5 percent to the bank. They couldn't get any credit elsewhere.

Then the world changed. The empire was dismantled,

loans went bad, customers stopped borrowing. The already overstaffed bank had to take on employees sent back from Prague or Cracow. The banks lost their profits and were eaten by their overhead costs.

This is Japan today.

Because of a practice dating to 1890 that obliges companies to hire from a list of universities to ensure a supply of graduates, businesses continued as recently as two years ago to hire even when business was declining. They were afraid they would be cut off the list of companies that would receive graduates.

I know one company that hired two hundred and eighty people from six universities, even though the company was shrinking.

So, the new hires sit around all day with nothing to do. In the evening they go out and get drunk with the boss. This is work?

How can Japan as a nineteenth-century European state make it in the hypercompetitive twenty-first century?

For all I have said, don't underrate the Japanese. They have an incredible ability to make brutal, 180-degree radical changes overnight. And since there is no tradition of compassion in Japan, the emotional scars of these changes are tremendous.

Though for four hundred years no non-European country had anywhere near the level of international trade Japan had, in 1637 they closed to the outside world. And they did it within six months. The dislocation was unbelievable.

In 1867, with the Meiji Restoration, they opened up again—overnight.

Nineteen forty-five was obviously a different story, as they were defeated in war.

When the dollar was devalued about ten years ago, the Japanese wasted no time moving manufacturing out of Japan to cheaper spots in Asia. They established partnerships with overseas Chinese and gained an almost unbeatable lead as producers in mainland China.

Japan is very capable of dramatic about-faces. Once they reach a certain critical mass of consensus, the change is very swift.

My guess is that it will take a major scandal to trigger change. A banking collapse may provide this. So far, they have been postponing tackling their weak financial system, hoping the problem would go away or could be liquidated step by step. But, as time goes on, it doesn't look like that is possible.

On China

Within the next ten years, China will have transformed itself. If history is any guide, it will segment into some kind of regional decentralization.

Today, we already have the so-called autonomous regions. In the old days they were called territories controlled by warlords.

Already, these regions pay more lip service than taxes

to Beijing. The only reason they don't openly break with the central government is because they want access to the huge subsidies for state industries.

Overhauling these thoroughly inefficient industries without provoking social upheaval is China's greatest hurdle in the times ahead.

The world's largest bicycle factory is in Xi'an. But the quality of these bikes is so poor that they fall apart if you look at them. So everyone in Xi'an rides Shanghai bicycles—even though their importation into Xi'an is supposedly forbidden.

Already, there are 5 million bikes lying around unsold in Xi'an. But they keep making more because 85,000 people are employed at the plant.

Once I spoke with the director of the famous Beijing Truck Plant No. 2. He told me that he had 115,000 people producing 45,000 trucks, but if he could only reduce his workforce to 45,000, he would be able to produce 115,000 trucks.

I saw in that plant machine tools that Ford had shipped to Shanghai in 1926. Then it had some unbelievably poor Russian equipment from the 1950s. Then it had three warehouses full of computer programming equipment in crates.

"Why don't you use these computers?" I asked the director. He told me that for six years he had requested money in his budget to translate the instructions into Chinese, but his request had not so far been granted.

This is like Russia in 1929–30 when tractors stood idle

in the fields because the ministry in charge didn't allow the import of spare parts such as fan belts.

There are three answers for China. The first answer is the official one: They will become efficient and modern. There are a few examples of this, like the Shanghai bicycle plant, but not many.

The second answer comes from an old Chinese saying, "To walk a straight line, fall off one side, then the other." In practice, this is what China has been doing for the last seven years. First, they finance their industries through inflationary subsidies until the danger of too much unemployment subsides. Then they whittle down the workforce at the big state industries a little more until there is again too much unemployment, then inflate again. Each time, they can cut back a little.

The third answer, which in many ways is the most realistic one, is to concentrate on a few areas where they can set enough examples of well-performing enterprises so that they can attract foreign capital. This has been the approach of the Shanghai region, and essentially, it has worked.

Overall, do you think the current crisis across Asia will result in a breakdown of the globalization process, or lead to its acceleration because of the need for foreign capital?

In the midst of crisis, continued economic liberalization is a pipe dream—and not just in Asia. Don't forget that economic liberalization means an immediate dislocation as against long-term improvement.

Look at France today. For 110 years, the unions have entertained the superstition that by cutting the workweek you will create more jobs. It has never worked where it has been tried. It is only going to make unemployment worse and no new jobs will be created.

All the experience during the 1920s and the Great Depression points to one unfortunate reality: Under the pressure of unemployment, nations don't open up. They close down.

If the mass production revolution of the twentieth century produced the basic disturbances that led to depression and war, will technological unemployment that comes as the result of the knowledge revolution be the basic disturbance of the twenty-first century?

I see no evidence of this. Since the advent of computers we have feared the unemployment effects of automation. But they haven't materialized.

In America, the land of Microsoft and Intel, unemployment has been at its lowest level in decades. If anything, Europe has such high unemployment because it has not adequately integrated information technology into society and it has not adjusted its rigid labor markets to the flexible mode of the knowledge age.

What, then, will be the "basic disturbance" of the twenty-first century as you see it?

The demographic challenge. In all the developed countries, the issue is not so much the one everybody talks about—the aging of the population—but the shrinking of the young population.

Business Opportunities

The U.S. is the only advanced country where there are enough babies—2.2 per woman of reproductive age—to replace the population. But only because of our high immigration. Among immigrant Latinos four children is still the norm.

(1998)

Part III

THE CHANGING WORLD ECONOMY

11

The Rise of the Great Institutions

The history of society in the West during the last millennium can—without much oversimplification—be summed up in one phrase: the rise, fall, and rise of pluralism.

By the year 1000 the West—that is, Europe north of the Mediterranean and west of Greek Orthodoxy—had become a startlingly new and distinct civilization and society, much later dubbed feudalism. At its core was the world's first, and all but invincible, fighting machine: the heavily armored knight fighting on horseback. What made possible fighting on horseback, and with it the armored knight, was the stirrup, an invention that had originated in Central Asia sometime around the year 600. The entire Old World had accepted the stirrup long before 1000;

everybody riding a horse anywhere in the Old World rode with a stirrup.

But every other Old World civilization—Islam, India, China, Japan—rejected what the stirrup made possible: fighting on horseback. And the reason these civilizations rejected it, despite its tremendous military superiority, was that the armored knight on horseback had to be an autonomous power center beyond the control of central government. To support a single one of these fighting machines—the knight and his three to five horses and their attendants; the five or more squires (knights in training) necessitated by the profession's high casualty rate; the unspeakably expensive armor—required the economic output of one hundred peasant families, that is of some five hundred people, about fifty times as many as were needed to support the best-equipped professional foot soldier, such as a Roman legionnaire or a Japanese samurai.

Control over the Fief

The knight exercised full political, economic, and social control over the entire knightly enterprise, the fief. This, in short order, induced every other unit in medieval Western society—secular or religious—to become an autonomous power center, paying lip service to a central authority such as the pope or a king, but certainly nothing else such as taxes. These separate power centers included barons and counts, bishops and the enormously wealthy monasteries, free cities and craft guilds, and a few decades later, the early universities and countless trading monopolies.

By 1066, when William the Conqueror's victory brought feudalism to England, the West had become totally pluralist. And every group tried constantly to gain more autonomy and more power: political and social control of its members and of access to the privileges membership conferred, its own judiciary, its own fighting force, the right to coin its own money, and so on. By 1200 these "special interests" had all but taken over. Every one of them pursued only its goals and was concerned only with its own aggrandizement, wealth, and power. No one was concerned with the common good; and the capacity to make societywide policy was all but gone.

The reaction began in the thirteenth century in the religious sphere, when—feebly at first—the papacy tried, at two councils in Lyon, France, to reassert control over bishops and monasteries. It finally established that control at the Council of Trent in the mid-sixteenth century, by which time the pope and the Catholic Church had lost both England and Northern Europe to Protestantism. In the secular sphere, the counterattack against pluralism began one hundred years later. The long bow—a Welsh invention perfected by the English—had by 1350 destroyed the knight's superiority on the battlefield. A few years later the cannon—adapting to military uses the powder the Chinese had invented for their fireworks—brought down the hitherto impregnable knight's castle.

From then on, for more than five hundred years, Western history is the history of the advance of the national state as the sovereign; that is, as the *only* power center in society. The process was very slow; the resistance of the entrenched "special interests" was enormous. It was not until 1648, for instance—in the Treaty of Westphalia, which ended Europe's Thirty Years' War—that private armies were abolished, with the nation-state acquiring a monopoly on maintaining armies and on fighting wars. But the process was steady. Step by step, pluralist institutions lost their autonomy. By the end of the Napoleonic Wars— or shortly thereafter—the sovereign national state had triumphed everywhere in Europe. Even the clergy in European countries had become civil servants, controlled by the state, paid by the state, and subject to the sovereign, whether king or parliament.

The one exception was the United States. Here pluralism survived—the main reason being America's almost unique religious diversity. And even in the United States, religiously grounded pluralism was deprived of power by the separation of church and state. It is no accident that in sharp contrast to continental Europe, no denominationally based party or movement has ever attracted more than marginal political support in the United States.

By the middle of the last century, social and political theorists, including Hegel and the liberal political philosophers of England and America, proclaimed proudly that pluralism was dead beyond redemption. And at that very moment it came back to life. The first organization that

178

had to have substantial power and substantial autonomy was the new business enterprise as it first arose, practically without precedent, between 1860 and 1870. It was followed in rapid order by a horde of other new institutions, scores of them by now, each requiring substantial autonomy and exercising considerable social control: the labor union, the civil service with its lifetime tenure, the hospital, the university. Each of them, like the pluralist institutions of eight hundred years ago, is a "special interest." Each needs—and fights for—its autonomy.

Not one of them is concerned with the common good. Consider what John L. Lewis, the powerful labor leader, said when Franklin D. Roosevelt asked him to call off a coal miners' strike that threatened to cripple the war effort: "The president of the United States is paid to look after the interest of the nation; I am paid to look after the interests of the coal miners." That is only an especially blunt version of what the leaders of every one of today's "special interests" believe—and what their constituents pay them for. As happened eight hundred years ago, this new pluralism threatens to destroy the capacity to make policy—and with it social cohesion altogether—in all developed countries.

But there is one essential difference between today's social pluralism and that of eight hundred years ago. Then, the pluralist institutions—knights in armor, free cities, merchant guilds, or "exempt" bishoprics—were based on property and power. Today's autonomous organization— business enterprise, labor union, university, hospital—is based on function. It derives its capacity to perform squarely from its narrow focus on its single function. The one major attempt to restore the power monopoly of the sovereign state, Stalin's Russia, collapsed primarily because none of its institutions, being deprived of the needed autonomy, could or did function—not even, it seems, the military, let alone businesses or hospitals.

Needed Autonomy

Only yesterday most of the tasks today's organizations discharge were supposed to be done by the family. The family educated its members. It took care of the old and the sick. It found work for members who needed it. And not one of these tasks was actually performed, as even the most cursory look at nineteenth-century family letters or family histories shows. These tasks can be accomplished only by a truly autonomous institution, independent from either the community or the state.

The challenge of the next millennium, or rather of the next century (we won't have a thousand years), is to preserve the autonomy of our institutions—and in some cases, like transnational business, autonomy over and beyond national sovereignties—while at the same time restoring the unity of the polity that we have all but lost, at least in peacetime. We can only hope this can be done— but so far no one yet knows *how* to do it. We do know that it will require something that is even less precedented than today's pluralism: the willingness and ability of each of today's institutions to maintain the focus on the narrow and specific function that gives them the capacity to perform, and yet the willingness and ability to work together and with political authority for the common good.

This is the enormous challenge the second millennium in the developed countries is bequeathing the third millennium.

(2000)

12

The Global Economy
and the Nation-State

A True Survivor

Long before talk of the globalization of the world's economy began some thirty-five years ago, the demise of the nation-state had been widely predicted. Actually, the best and the brightest have been predicting the nation-state's demise for two hundred years, beginning with Immanuel Kant in his 1795 essay "Perpetual Peace," through Karl Marx in "Withering Away of the State," to Bertrand Russell's speeches in the 1950s and 1960s. The latest such prediction by eminent and serious people appears in a book called *The Sovereign Individual* by Lord William Rees-Mogg, former editor of the London *Times* and now vice chairman of the BBC, and James Dale Davidson, chairman of Britain's National Tax Payers' Union. Rees-Mogg and Davidson assert that for all but the lowest earners the Internet will make avoiding taxes so easy and riskless that sovereignty will inevitably shift to the individual, leaving the nation-state to die of fiscal starvation.

Despite all its shortcomings, the nation-state has shown amazing resilience. While Czechoslovakia and Yugoslavia have been casualties of a changing order, Turkey, a nation that never before existed as such, has become a functioning nation-state. India, rarely united except under a foreign conqueror, is holding together as a nation-state. And every country that emerged from the nineteenth-century colonial empires has established itself as a nation-state, as have all the countries emerging from the breakup of the Eurasian empire forged by the czars and tied together even more tightly by the czar's communist successors. So far, at least, there is no other institution capable of political integration and effective membership in the world's political community. In all probability, therefore, the nation-state will survive the globalization of the economy and the Information Revolution that accompanies it. But it will be a greatly changed nation-state, especially in domestic fiscal and monetary policies, foreign economic policies, control of international business, and, perhaps, in its conduct of war.

The Nation-State Afloat

Control of money, credit, and fiscal policy was one of the three pillars on which Jean Bodin, the brilliant French lawyer who coined the term *sovereignty,* set the nation-state in his 1576 *Six Books of the Republic.* It has never been a sturdy pillar. By the late nineteenth century, the dominant currency was no longer state-minted coins or state-printed banknotes, but credit created by fast-growing privately controlled commercial banks. The nation-state countered with the central bank. By 1912, when the United States established the Federal Reserve System, every nation-state had its own central bank to control the commercial banks and their credit. But throughout the nineteenth century, one nation-state after another put itself (or was put) under the control of the nonnational gold standard, which imposed strict limits on a country's monetary and fiscal policies. And the gold exchange standard, established in the Bretton Woods agreements after World War II, while a good deal more flexible than the pre–World War I gold standard, still did not give individual countries full monetary and fiscal sovereignty. Only in 1973, when President Nixon floated the U.S. dollar, did the nation-state—or so it was claimed—attain full autonomy in monetary and fiscal affairs. Surely governments and their economists had learned enough to use such sovereignty responsibly.

185

Not many economists—at least in the English-speaking world—want to go back to fixed exchange rates or anything resembling the old system. But even fewer would claim that nation-states have shown skill or responsibility in using their new fiscal and monetary freedom. Floating currencies, it was promised, would make for stable currencies, with the market controlling exchange rates through constant small adjustments. Instead, there has been no period in peacetime, save the early years of the Great Depression, in which currencies have fluctuated as widely and abruptly as since 1973. Freed from external constraints, governments have gone on spending binges.

The Bundesbank in Germany is practically free from political control and is dedicated to fiscal rectitude. It knew that the spending spree the politicians proposed during the country's reunification was economic folly, and it said so loud and clear. Still the politicians went ahead, gaining short-term popularity while risking long-term economic costs. The Bundesbank predicted everything that has come to pass, including unemployment rates in both East and West Germany not seen since the dying days of the Weimar Republic. It is the same with politicians everywhere; it makes little difference which party is in power or how much it promises to cut or control.

Virtual Money

While the hope that governments will practice self-discipline is fantasy, the global economy imposes new and more severe restraints on government. It is forcing government back into fiscal responsibility. Floating exchange rates have created extreme currency instability, which in turn has created an enormous mass of "world money." This money has no existence outside the global economy and its main money markets. It is not being created by economic activity like investment, production, consumption, or trade. It is created primarily by currency trading. It fits none of the traditional definitions of money, whether standard of measurement, storage of value, or medium of exchange. It is totally anonymous. It is virtual rather than real money.

But its power is real. The volume of world money is so gigantic that its movements in and out of a currency have far greater impact than the flows of trade, or investment. In one day, as much of this virtual money may be traded as the entire world needs to finance trade and investment for a year. This virtual money has total mobility because it serves no economic function. Billions of it can be switched from one currency to another by a trader pushing a few buttons on a keyboard. And because it serves no economic function and finances nothing, this money also does not follow economic logic or rationality.

It is volatile and easily panicked by a rumor or unexpected event.

One example is the run on the dollar in the spring of 1995, which forced President Clinton to abandon his earlier spending plans and embrace a balanced budget. The run was triggered by the failure of the Republican majority in the Senate to pass a constitutional amendment calling for a balanced budget. Even if the amendment had passed, it would have been meaningless. It was riddled with loopholes and required ratification by thirty-eight states to become law, which at best would have taken many years. But the world's currency traders panicked and started a run on the U.S. dollar. Already undervalued 10 percent against the Japanese yen, the run pushed the dollar down another 25 percent—from 106 yen to the dollar to less than 80—in two weeks. More important, the run caused the near collapse of the U.S. bond market, on which the United States depends to finance its deficits. The central banks of the United States, England, Germany, Japan, Switzerland, and France instantly swung into concerted action to support the dollar. They failed, losing billions in the attempt. It took the dollar the better part of a year to climb back to its original (still undervalued) exchange rate.

A similar panic-driven run on the French franc in 1981 forced President Mitterrand to abandon promises that had helped get him elected three months earlier. There have been panic runs on the Swedish krona, the British pound, the Italian lira, and the Mexican peso. Virtual money won every time, proving that the global economy is the ultimate arbiter of monetary and fiscal policies.

Currency runs, however, are not the appropriate cure for fiscal irresponsibility. In the case of Mexico, they were worse than the disease. The 1995 run on the peso wiped out six years of hard-won economic gains that had turned the country from a basket case into an emerging economy. But so far there is no other control on fiscal irresponsibility. The only thing that can work is fiscal and monetary policies that free a country from depending on borrowing short-term, volatile world money to cover its deficits. This is likely to require a balanced budget—or something very close to balanced—over any three- or five-year period. And this then puts severe limitations on the nation-state's fiscal and monetary autonomy, which the 1973 floating of exchange rates was supposed to set free for all time.

The process of restoring such nonnational and supranational restraints is well under way. The Eurobank's currency for the entire European Economic Community, planned to be in place before the century's end, would transfer control of money and credit from the individual member states to an independent transnational agency. Another approach, apparently favored by the U.S. Federal Reserve Board, would give a consortium of central banks similar authority, thus maintaining the trappings of national fiscal sovereignty while taking away much of its reality. Both approaches, however, would only institutionalize what has already become an economic reality: Basic economic decisions are made in and by the global economy rather than the nation-state.

The unrestrained financial and monetary sovereignty given to the nation-state by floating exchange rates twenty-five years ago has not been good for government. It has largely deprived government of its ability to say no. It has transferred decision-making power from government to special interest groups. It is largely to blame for the precipitate decline in confidence in and respect for government that has been a conspicuous and disturbing trend in almost every country. Paradoxically, losing its fiscal and monetary sovereignty may make the nation-state stronger rather than weaker.

Breaking the Rules

Far subtler but perhaps even more important is the impact of the global economy's rise on the basic assumptions and theories on which most governments, especially in the West, base their international economic policies. There are any number of signs that something is going on in the world economy that breaks the rules that have been at work for decades.

Why did the dollar fall against the yen by more than 50 percent when President Reagan and the Japanese government agreed to give up the fixed 250:1 yen-to-dollar rate in 1983? While the dollar was indeed overvalued, its purchasing-power parity with the yen was around 230. No one expected it to drop below 200 yen. Instead, the dollar went into free fall and did not come to rest until it had lost almost 60 percent of its value against the yen, that is, until it hit 110 yen two years later (only to fall again ten years later to 80 yen). Why? To this day, there has been no explanation. Even more mysterious, the dollar showed such a sharp fall only against the yen. In fact, it increased its value against some other key currencies. Again, no one anticipated this and no one can explain it.

Reagan and his economic advisers wanted a cheaper dollar so as to eliminate a growing trade deficit with Japan. According to all theory and two hundred years of experience, a lower dollar should mean more American exports to Japan and fewer American imports from Japan. Japanese exporters, especially the automobile and consumer electronics manufacturers, went into hysterics and announced that the end of the world had come. American exports did indeed go up sharply, but even more to some countries against whose currencies the dollar gained in value. But Japanese exports to the United States, despite the dollar depreciation, rose even faster than U.S. exports to Japan, so that the U.S. trade deficit with Japan actually went up rather than down. Every time in the last fifteen years that the dollar has slid against the yen, the American administration of the day has predicted that Japan's trade surplus with the United States would shrink. Every time the Japanese have screamed that they were ruined. And every time Japan's export surplus has increased almost immediately.

One popular explanation is that Japanese manufacturers are geniuses. But although the major exporters are very sharp, genius cannot overcome a 50 percent drop in revenues in virtually no time. The true explanation is that Japan benefited as much from the lower dollar as it was penalized by it. Japan is the world's largest importer of foodstuffs and raw materials, all of which are priced in dollars. It spends roughly as much on importing these commodities as it earns dollars by exporting finished manufactured goods. An individual Japanese manufacturing company like Toyota may lose because the dollars it gets for its cars exported to the United States earn only half as many yen as before, but for the entire Japanese economy the drop in the dollar's value against the yen was simply a wash.

But this raises another, even more mysterious riddle. What explains why the Japanese did not have to pay more for the commodities they imported? According to all theory and earlier experience, commodity prices in dollars should have gone up as much as the dollar went down. The Japanese should have had to pay as much as they did before the dollar was devalued. If that had happened, as it always had before, there would indeed be no Japanese surplus in trade with the United States. But commodity prices in dollars today are lower than in 1983—and there is no explanation for this either.

There is only one piece of the puzzle that makes sense, but it is even less compatible with traditional international trade theory. The U.S. Department of Commerce estimates that 40 percent or more of goods exported from any developed country go to overseas subsidiaries and affiliates of domestic companies. Officially and legally, they are exports. Economically, they are intracompany transfers. They are machines, supplies, and half-finished goods that have been engineered into the production of the plant or the affiliate abroad and must be continued, whatever the exchange rate. To change this relationship would take years and cost more than foreign exchange savings could possibly recover. Forty percent of what is reported as trade in goods is thus "trade" only as a legal fiction. And that proportion is steadily growing.

International trade theory takes for granted that investment follows trade. Most people think "international trade in goods" when they hear the words *international trade.* But increasingly today, trade follows investment. International movements of capital rather than international movements of goods have become the engine of the world economy. And while trade in goods has indeed grown faster since World War II than in any other period in history, trade in services has been growing even faster, whether it be financial services, management consulting, accounting, insurance, or retailing. Service exports twenty years ago were so small that they were rarely recorded in trade statistics. Today they are a quarter of U.S. exports and the only producers of sizable American export surpluses.

They follow few, if any, of the rules of traditional international trade. Only tourism, for instance, is highly sensitive to foreign exchange rates and their fluctuations.

I have intentionally stuck to American economic conundrums, but similar ones can be found in the economy of every developed country and most developing countries. The centers of the world economy have shifted away from the developed countries. Only fifteen years ago it was generally believed that the growth of developing countries depended on the prosperity of the developed ones. In the last two decades, the developed countries have not done particularly well; but world trade and production have boomed as never before, with the bulk of the growth occurring in emerging countries. The explanation, in large part, is that knowledge has replaced the economist's "land, labor, and capital" as the chief economic resource. Knowledge, mainly in the form of the training methods and philosophies developed in the United States during World War II, exploded the axiom that low wages mean low productivity. Training now enables a country's labor force to attain world-class productivity while still paying an emerging country's wages for at least eight or ten years.

These new realities require different economic theories and different international economic policies. Even if a lower exchange rate improves a country's exports, it also weakens a country's ability to invest abroad. And if trade follows investment, lower foreign exchange rates for a country's currency diminish exports within a few years.

This is what happened to the United States: The cheaper dollar increased American manufactured exports in the short term. But it also impaired the ability of American industry to invest abroad and thus to create export markets for the long term. As a result, the Japanese are now far ahead of the Americans in market share and market leadership in the emerging countries of East and Southeast Asia.

The need for new theories and policies explains the sudden interest in what is being promoted by James Fallows, editor in chief of *U.S. News and World Report,* and others as the "national development policies" of the nineteenth-century German economist Friedrich R. List. Actually, the policies List preached in 1830s Germany protection of infant industries so as to develop domestic business—were not List's and were not German. They are strictly American, growing out of Alexander Hamilton's 1791 "Report on Manufactures," which Henry Clay, twenty-five years later, expanded into what he called the American System. List, in the United States as a political refugee from Germany, learned them while serving as Clay's secretary.

What makes these old ideas attractive is that Hamilton, Clay, and List did not focus on trade. They were neither free traders nor protectionists. They focused on investment. Asian economies, beginning with Japan after World War II, have been following policies similar to those Hamilton and Clay advocated for the infant United States. The international economic policies likely to emerge over the next generation will be neither free-trade nor protectionist, but focused on investment rather than trade.

Selling to the World

In the global economy, businesses are increasingly forced to shift from being multinational to being transnational. The traditional multinational is a national company with foreign subsidiaries. These subsidiaries are clones of the parent company. A German subsidiary of an American manufacturing company, say, is a self-contained operation that manufactures almost everything it sells within Germany, buying its supplies there and employing almost exclusively Germans.

Most companies doing international business today are still organized as traditional multinationals. But the transformation into transnational companies has begun, and it is moving fast. The products or services may be the same, but the structure is fundamentally different. In a transnational company there is only one economic unit, the world. Selling, servicing, public relations, and legal affairs are local. But parts, machines, planning, research, finance, marketing, pricing, and management are conducted in contemplation of the world market. One of America's leading engineering companies, for instance, makes one critical part for all of its forty-three plants worldwide in one location outside of Antwerp, Belgium—and nothing else. It has organized product development for the entire world in three places and quality control in four. For this company, national boundaries have largely become irrelevant.

The transnational company is not totally beyond the control of national governments. It must adapt to them. But these adaptations are exceptions to policies and practices decided on for worldwide markets and technologies. Successful transnational companies see themselves as separate, nonnational entities. This self-perception is evidenced by something unthinkable a few decades ago: a transnational top management. The world's best-known management consulting firm, McKinsey & Co., for instance, though headquartered in New York, is headed by an Indian. And for many years the number two man at Citibank, the only big commercial bank that has gone transnational, was Chinese.

The U.S. government is trying to counteract this trend by extending American legal concepts and legislation beyond its shores. It is doing so with respect to antitrust laws, an almost uniquely American concept. It is also trying to rein in transnational companies through American laws covering torts, product liability, and corruption. And America goes to battle against transnational companies through economic sanctions against Cuba and Iraq.

Although the United States is still the world's largest economic power—and likely to remain so for many years—the attempt to mold the world economy to American moral, legal, and economic concepts is futile. In a global economy in which major players can emerge almost overnight, there can be no dominant economic power.

Nonetheless, there is certainly need for moral, legal, and economic rules that are accepted and enforced throughout the global economy. A central challenge, therefore, is the development of international law and supranational organizations that can make and enforce rules for the global economy.

War After Global Economics

Though incompatible, the global economy and total war are both children of this century. The strategic goal in traditional warfare, in Clausewitz's famous phrase, was "to destroy the enemy's fighting forces." War was to be waged against the enemy's soldiers. It was not supposed to be waged against enemy civilians and their property. There were always exceptions, of course. Sherman's march through Georgia at the end of the U.S. Civil War was aimed at civilians and their property rather than the threadbare Confederate army. But that it was an exception—and meant to be one—is one reason it is still so vividly remembered. A few years later, in the Franco-Prussian War of 1870–71, Bismarck took great care to keep France's financial system intact.

But during this century's first war, the Boer War, the rule was changed. The goal of warfare was redefined as destroying the enemy's potential for waging war, which meant destroying the enemy's economy. Also, for the first time in modern Western history, war was systematically waged against the enemy's civilian population. To break the fighting spirit of the Boer soldiers, the British herded Boer women and children into history's first concentration camps.

Before this century, the West generally observed another rule: Enemy civilians residing in one's country were to be left unmolested so long as they did not engage in political activity. But in World War I, Britain and France interned all enemy aliens, although the United States, Germany, and Austria refrained. Until 1900, businesses and property owned by foreign nationals or by companies domiciled in an enemy country were left undisturbed. Since World War I—with the British again taking the lead—such property was confiscated and put under government custodianship in wartime.

The rules of total war are so firmly established by now that most people take them to be akin to laws of nature. With missiles, satellites, and nuclear weapons, there can be no return to the nineteenth-century belief that the military's first task is to keep war away from the country's civilians. In modern war, there are no civilians.

But while destroying the enemy's economy helps win the war, it impairs the victor's chance of winning the peace. This was one of the most significant lessons of this century's two postwar periods, the twenty years after 1918 and the fifty years after 1945. The unprecedented American policies after World War II, including the Marshall

Plan, brought about the speedy recovery of the former enemy economies, and with them fifty years of unprecedented economic expansion and prosperity for the victors as well. These policies came into existence because George Marshall, Harry Truman, Dean Acheson, and Douglas MacArthur remembered the catastrophic consequences of World War I's punitive peace. If "war is the continuation of policy by other means," to quote another maxim from Clausewitz, then total war will have to be adjusted to the realities of the global economy.

Since businesses are moving from multinational to transnational, total-war doctrines may actually be detrimental to a country's war effort these days. For example, Italy's largest armaments producer during World War I was an automobile company named Fiat. Austria-Hungary's largest armaments producer in its fight against Italy during World War I was the wholly owned Austrian subsidiary of Fiat. It had been founded a year or two after the parent company started in Italy, but by 1914 it was substantially larger and more advanced than its parent, owing to the greater size of Austria-Hungary's market. To make this Italian-owned subsidiary the center of Austria's war production required literally nothing but a new bank account.

Today such a wholly owned subsidiary would assemble and sell whole cars, but might only manufacture brakes. That subsidiary's brakes would be used by all the company's plants worldwide, and it would receive all the other parts and supplies it needed from other subsidiaries throughout the world. This transnational integration could cut the costs of the finished automobile by as much as 50 percent. But it also makes an individual subsidiary practically unable to produce anything if cut off from the rest of the company. In many developed countries, businesses integrated transnationally now account for one-third to one-half of their industry's output.

I do not pretend to know the answers to the growing contradiction between peacetime and wartime economies. But there is a precedent. The most innovative political achievement of the nineteenth century was the International Red Cross. First proposed in 1862 by a Swiss citizen, Jean Henri Dunant, it became the world's first transnational agency within ten years and it is still the world's most successful one. What it did in setting universal rules for treating the wounded and prisoners of war may need to be done now with respect to the treatment of civilians and their property. That, too, in all likelihood, will require a transnational agency and, as in the case of the Red Cross, substantial curtailment of national sovereignty.

Since the early Industrial Revolution, it has been argued that economic interdependence would prove stronger than nationalist passions. Kant was the first to say so. The "moderates" of 1860 believed it until the first shots were fired at Fort Sumter. The Liberals of Austria-Hungary believed to the very end that their economy was far too integrated to be split into separate countries. So, quite clearly, did Mikhail Gorbachev. But whenever in the last two hundred years political passions and nation-state politics have collided with economic rationality, political passions and the nation-state have won.

(1997)

13

It's the Society, Stupid

A Heretic's View

American policy on Japan, especially during Asia's economic crisis, is based on five assumptions that have become articles of faith for most American policymakers, Japan scholars, and even a good many business executives. But all of them are either plain wrong or, at best, highly dubious:

1. The government bureaucracy's dominance is assumed to be unique to Japan, like its near monopoly on policymaking and its control of business

and the economy through "administrative guidance."

2. Reducing the bureaucracy's role to what it should be—"the expert is on tap but not on top"—would not be that difficult. All that is needed is political will.

3. A ruling elite like the Japanese bureaucracy is both unnecessary in a modern developed society and undesirable in a democracy.

4. The Japanese bureaucracy's resistance to "deregulation," especially now in the financial sector, is nothing but a selfish clinging to power that will do severe damage. By delaying the inevitable, it can only make things worse.

5. Finally, the Japanese—they are intelligent people, after all—put the economy first, as we do.

The right assumptions about Japan, however, are:

1. Bureaucracies dominate almost all developed countries. The United States and a few less populous English-speaking countries such as Australia, New Zealand, and Canada are the exceptions rather than the rule. Indeed, the Japanese bureaucracy is a good deal less overbearing than that of some other developed countries, particularly France.

2. Bureaucratic elites have far greater staying power than we are willing to concede. They manage

to keep power for decades despite scandals and proven incompetence.

3. This is because developed countries—with the sole exception of the United States—are convinced that they need a ruling elite, without which they fear social disintegration. As such, they cling to the old elite unless there is a universally accepted replacement, and no such replacement is in sight in Japan.

4. Their experience has proven to the Japanese that procrastination works. Twice during the last forty years, Japan has overcome major and apparently insoluble social problems not by "solving" them but by delaying until, in the end, the problems evaporated. The procrastination strategy will probably fail this time, considering the shaky structure and solvency of Japan's financial system. Given Japan's earlier experiences, however, procrastination is not an irrational strategy.

5. In fact, it is the logical strategy since for the Japanese policymaker—whether politician, civil servant, or leading business executive—society comes first, not the economy.

Descending from Heaven

Descent from heaven—the Japanese term for the practice whereby senior civil servants, having reached their terminal government position around age forty-five to fifty-five, become "counselors" to big companies—is seen in the United States as uniquely Japanese. The shift is considered the most visible manifestation of the dominance, power, and privilege of the Japanese bureaucracy. But it is actually a universal custom in all developed countries, including the United States.

To use a personal example, my father was the civil service head of the Austrian Ministry of Commerce just after World War I. When he retired in 1923, not yet fifty, he was promptly appointed chairman and CEO of a big bank, as were his predecessor and his successor. So were their counterparts in the Ministry of Finance. Senior Austrian civil servants in key ministries "descend from heaven" to this day.

Japanese counselors who descend from heaven are well paid, but the job is a sinecure. They are usually not even expected to show up at the company's office except to collect their paychecks once a month. By contrast, in most European countries these "retiring" civil servants move into real jobs, as did the Austrian civil servants who became bank CEOs.

Whether this is wise or foolish is beside the point. Such practices are universal. In Germany the second-tier civil servant who will not make it into a top position in a ministry becomes secretary-general of an industry association, a job that not only pays well but has real power. Membership in such associations is compulsory in Germany, and all but the very largest companies must conduct their relations with both government and labor unions through them. If the civil servant is a Social Democrat, he gets a similar job—equally well paid and powerful—as chief economist or secretary-general of a labor union. In France, the civil servant who has reached the exalted position of *inspecteur de finance,* usually around age forty or forty-five, moves into a top position in industry or finance. Almost every power position in the French economy and society is filled by a former *inspecteur de finance.* Even in the United Kingdom, it remains customary for the top civil servant in a major ministry to chair a big bank or insurance company after his retirement.

In the United States, too, "descending from heaven" is anything but unknown. Scores of generals and admirals have, upon retirement, taken senior executive positions in defense and aerospace companies. An even larger number of congressional staffers and political appointees in the upper and middle levels of executive agencies—together, Washington's ruling elite—routinely come from on high to become well-paid lobbyists or partners in Washington law firms.

Even at the peak of its power circa 1970, the Japanese bureaucracy still had less control of business and the economy than its European counterparts. In both France and Germany, the government directly owns large chunks of the economy. A fifth of Europe's largest automobile producer, Volkswagen, is owned by the state of Saxony, giving it absolute veto power. Until quite recently, the French government owned most of the country's major banks and insurance companies. The same is true in Italy, the third-largest economy on the Continent. Japan, by contrast, owns almost nothing of the economy besides the Postal Savings Bank. Where the Japanese make do with "administrative guidance," or control through persuasion, the Europeans rely on *dirigisme*, direct decision-making power as owners and managers, for good or ill.

Elites Rule

How difficult could it be to curtail the Japanese bureaucrats' power? After all, the bureaucracy's record is dismal. It reeled from one failure after another for the past twenty-five years. It failed miserably to pick the winners in the late 1960s and early 1970s, choosing instead such losers as the mainframe supercomputer. As a result, Japan today lags far behind in the information industry and in high-tech altogether.

The bureaucracy failed again in the 1980s. Panicked by a mild recession, it plunged Japan into the wild excess of the speculative fiscal bubble and with it into the present financial crisis. "Administrative guidance" pushed banks, insurance companies, and businesses into stock and real estate investments at insanely inflated prices and into the worst kind of problem loans. When the bubble burst in the early 1990s, the bureaucracy could not get Japan's economy going again. It poured unprecedented amounts of money—far beyond anything the U.S. government tried during the New Deal—into attempts to raise stock prices, real estate prices, consumption, and capital investment, all without any effect. In 1997, the bureaucracy followed that up by totally failing to anticipate the financial crisis in mainland Asia. It still urged Japanese banks and industry to invest more money in Asia even after mainland economies began to totter.

Since then, the bureaucracy has been revealed to be riddled with corruption, even prestigious agencies such as the Bank of Japan or the Ministry of Finance. This cost the bureaucrats their claim to moral leadership. Even the bureaucracy's staunchest supporters, the big companies, have turned against it. Big business's organization, the Keidanren, is now calling for deregulation and clipping the bureaucracy's wings.

Yet nothing happens. Worse, even the tiny, timid, token gestures by politicians to assert control over the bureaucracy, like kicking a powerful bureaucrat upstairs, are quietly reversed a few weeks later. There is, Americans argue, something unusual going on, something "exceptionally Japanese."

But ruling elites—especially those which, like Japan's, are based not on birth or wealth but on function—have remarkable staying power. They remain in power long after they have lost credibility and public respect. Consider the French military. This ruling elite's pretensions were shattered when the Dreyfus scandal of the 1890s showed it to be corrupt, dishonorable, dishonest, and bereft of the "military virtues" that underlie an army's claim to social leadership. Yet it held on to power, even after its abysmal incompetence in World War I proved it capable only of senseless mass slaughter. Totally discredited, especially in the years of widespread West European pacifism after the Great War, it had enough strength in 1936 to defeat an attempt by Léon Blum's government to shift power to a civil service elite. Teaming up with the French communists, the military forced Blum from power. And in 1940, even after it had again proven its utter incompetence by inflicting on France the most humiliating defeat the country had ever suffered, the French military still had enough power to make the Vichy collaborators choose the least discredited of France's military leaders, the nearly senile Marshal Pétain, to win legitimacy and widespread popular support for their puppet regime.

The extraordinary ability of a ruling elite to stalemate any attempt to unhorse it is by no means a Japanese phenomenon. Developed countries, especially developed democracies, are convinced that they need a ruling elite. Without it, society and politics disintegrate—as, in turn, does democracy. Only the United States and the few smaller English-speaking countries are immune to this certainty. American society has not had a ruling elite since the early years of the nineteenth century. Indeed, as almost every foreign observer of America since Tocqueville has remarked, the truly unique feature of U.S. society is that every group feels itself unappreciated, disrespected, if not discriminated against—a feature many of us consider the country's greatest strength. But America is the exception. Japan is the rule. In all major developed countries other than the United States, it is considered self-evident that without a ruling elite there can be neither political stability nor social order.

Consider Charles de Gaulle and Konrad Adenauer. Both had been outsiders rejected by the ruling elites of their societies—the French military and German governmental service, respectively. Despite their talents, they were denied preferment and power. De Gaulle did not make general until World War II broke out and even then got only the command of a small brigade. Adenauer was generally recognized as the country's most adroit politician and as an exceptionally able administrator, but he was never offered a cabinet appointment, let alone the chancellorship, for which he was clearly vastly more qualified than Weimar's mediocrities. Both men were bitter about their rejection by the elite, of which both were openly contemptuous. Yet both, upon winning power after the war, immediately set about creating a new ruling elite.

One of de Gaulle's first acts upon becoming president in 1945 was to make a new French civil service the elite it is today by melding a fractured mess of competing bureaucracies into one centrally controlled body, giving the civil servants control of all major positions in government and the economy, making the *inspecteurs de finance* all-powerful, and finally, creating a new credential, graduation from a new elite school, the École Nationale d'Administration. Out of it, for the last forty years, has come almost every social, political, or business leader in France, including, of course, practically all *inspecteurs de finance.*

When Adenauer became Germany's chancellor in 1949, he inherited a discredited, demoralized civil service deeply tainted by its subservience to the Nazis. Adenauer immediately set out to restore its elite status. He had himself been twice imprisoned by the Nazis, but despite heavy pressure, especially from the British and Americans, he shielded the civil service from de-Nazification. He restored its job security and the privileges the Nazis had abolished and gave it unprecedented freedom from interference by local politicians. Adenauer thereby gave the German civil service elite greater status than it ever had before, and this time it was not outranked by the military, as it had been under the kaiser and even in the Weimar Republic.

Both de Gaulle and Adenauer were denounced as undemocratic, and both responded by asserting that a modern society—and especially a modern democracy—disintegrates without a ruling elite. They had a point. In Weimar Germany, for one, the military was discredited by the defeat in World War I, although it did retain a veto. The civil service, which before 1918 had run a weak second to the army, was bitterly divided over whether to accept the republic. The new groups on the public stage, such as business leaders and professionals, were still seen as upstarts. The resulting absence of an accepted ruling group proved critical to the disintegration of Weimar. To take another example, the absence of a ruling elite surely has had something to do with Italy's political paralysis and social anomie.

The ruling elites that developed countries need to survive do, of course, cling to power. All rulers do. But elites can maintain themselves in power only because no replacement is in sight. Until such an alternative is provided—and it apparently takes a de Gaulle or an Adenauer to do so—the ruling elite will stay on, even if it is totally discredited and dysfunctional.

No replacement is in sight in Japan. The military, historically the ruling elite (indeed, the militarist regime of the 1930s was largely a replay of the shogunates, the military dictatorships that ruled Japan for most of its history), enjoys no public support whatsoever. Big business now commands unprecedented public respect, but it would not be accepted as society's ruling elite. Nor would the professoriate or professionals. So far the bureaucracy, no matter how discredited, is the only group that fits the bill. Whether America's policymakers like or dislike these facts is irrelevant. They are facts. American policy toward Japan must be based on the assumption that the bureaucracy will remain for the foreseeable future Japan's ruling elite, or at least its most powerful one—"deregulation" or not.

A Policy About Nothing

Japan's ruling elite does not behave like its rough equivalents in America. American elite groups are political: executive branch appointees and congressional staffers (both, incidentally, uniquely American phenomena alien to the rest of the developed world). But the ruling group in Japan is a bureaucracy, and it acts like one.

Max Weber, the great German sociologist who identified bureaucracy as a universal phenomenon, defined its function as codifying its experiences and converting them into rules of behavior. Three formative experiences in the collective memory of today's Japanese bureaucracy, two successes and one failure, provide the basis for its actions, especially in a major crisis.

The first success was not intervening in the most serious social malady of post–1945 Japan: the problem of an unemployed and unemployable rural majority. Today working farmers in both the United States and Japan make up no more than 2 or 3 percent of the workforce. In 1950, more than 20 percent of U.S. workers were farmers, but in Japan some 60 percent of the population was still living on the land, earning at best a bare subsistence. Most Japanese farmers in the early 1950s were utterly unproductive. Yet the bureaucracy successfully resisted all pressures to have government do anything about the farm problem. "Yes," it in effect admitted, "this enormous and totally unproductive overpopulation on the farms is a tremendous obstacle to economic development. Yes," it conceded, "subsidizing these farmers for producing nothing heavily penalizes the Japanese consumer at a time when most Japanese city dwellers are barely earning enough to pay for necessities." But doing anything to encourage farmers to move off the land or become more productive (which, in many cases, would have meant growing new crops like sorghum or soybeans, or moving out of growing rice and into breeding chicken and livestock) might cause serious social disruption. The only sensible thing to do, the bureaucracy argued, is absolutely nothing—and that is what it did.

Economically, Japan's farm policy has been a disaster. Agriculturally, Japan is worse off than any other developed country. It pays its remaining farmers as much in subsidies as do other developed countries, including the United States, but unlike the others, Japan now needs to import more of its food than ever before—more than any other major developed country. But socially, doing nothing has been a huge success. Japan has proportionately absorbed more former farmers into the urban population than any other developed country without the slightest social disruption.

The second great success of the Japanese bureaucracy was also a case of studied inaction: not tackling the problem of retail distribution. In the late 1950s and early 1960s, Japan had the most antiquated, expensive, and inefficient distribution system in the developed world—

more eighteenth-century than nineteenth-century. It consisted of thousands of "mom-and-pop" shops—tiny holes-in-the-wall with such enormous costs and outrageously high margins that each sold barely enough to let the owners scrape by. Economists and business leaders warned that Japan could not have a healthy modern economy until it had an efficient distribution system. The bureaucracy, however, refused to help. On the contrary, it passed regulation after regulation to slow the growth of modern retailers like supermarkets and discounters. "Economically," the bureaucrats agreed, "the existing retail system is an enormous drag. But it is Japan's social safety net. A person who loses his job or is retired at age fifty-five with just a few months' severance pay can always get a job at subsistence pay in his cousin's mom-and-pop shop." After all, Japan at that time still had no unemployment insurance or pensions.

Forty years later, the problem of retail distribution has disappeared, both socially and economically. The mom-and-pop shops are still there, but most, especially in the larger cities, have become franchisees of big new retail chains. The dank old stores are gone. Today's small shops are clean, well-lit, centrally managed, and computerized. Japan may well now have the world's most efficient and cheapest distribution system, and mom and pop now earn good money.

The third formative experience of the Japanese bureaucracy—unlike the first two, a gross failure—also taught it not to act. Indeed, this failure resulted from violating the above lessons and disregarding the wisdom of procrastination and delay. In the early 1980s, Japan had what in most parts of the world would not even be considered a recession but a mild slowdown in economic and employment growth. But this slowdown coincided with the uncoupling of the fixed dollar-yen exchange rate and a rapid fall in the exchange value of the U.S. dollar that panicked export-dependent Japan. The bureaucrats caved in under the resulting public pressure and became Western-style activists. They poured huge sums into attempts to stimulate the economy. Disaster ensued. The government began to run up larger budget deficits than most developed countries; the stock market boomed crazily, driving prices up to price-to-earning ratios of fifty to one or higher; there was an even wilder boom in urban real estate prices; and banks, swamped by money for which there were no solid borrowers, lent frenetically to speculators. The bubble burst, of course—the present financial crisis is its legacy—with banks, insurance companies, and thrifts drowning in stock market and real estate losses and uncollectible problem loans.

Subsequent events only confirmed the bureaucracy's conviction that procrastination is wiser than action. For again, in the last two years, due in some measure to pressure from Washington, Japanese politicians and public opinion have pushed the government to pour larger amounts of money into the economy than any other Western country, to absolutely no avail.

The Social Contract

The way the Japanese bureaucracy is now tackling—or, rather, not tackling—the Japanese banking system's crisis is commonly seen by Westerners as mere political cowardice, especially by official Washington: the U.S. Treasury, the World Bank, and the International Monetary Fund. But to Tokyo's ruling coterie, procrastination and delay appear the only rational policies.

No one knows yet how much Japanese financial institutions have suffered from the bursting of the bubble. On top of their domestic losses now loom huge additional losses inflicted by the economic crisis in other Asian countries—South Korea, Thailand, Indonesia, and Malaysia—where Japan's banks were by far the heaviest lenders, as they have also been to China.

Japan faces the largest financial crisis of any developed country since World War II. According to an estimate last May in *Business Week,* the Japanese banking system will eventually have to write off domestic losses of about $1 trillion, not including losses on loans and investment elsewhere in Asia. This sum handily tops even the highest estimate of the losses incurred in the U.S. savings and loan debacle fifteen years ago, and this in an economy barely half the size of America's. It amounts to a stunning 12 percent or so of the funds of all Japanese financial institutions.

Even more serious—and much harder to handle—are

the banking crisis's social threats. The entire Japanese financial system is already being radically downsized. Japan is grossly overbanked, not so much in the number of institutions as in the number of bank branches, which are both ubiquitous and heavily overstaffed. Japanese and American financial experts estimate that Japan's commercial banks employ three to five times as many people per thousand transactions as do American or European banks. This has made the banking system one of Japan's largest employers, as well as its highest-paying. Most of the redundant though well-paid employees are middle-aged people with limited skills who would find it hard to get other jobs if laid off. Unemployment in Japan has already risen to the highest levels in forty years—above 4 percent by the official count, and if Japan used American or European definitions of unemployment, it would be 7 or 8 percent. Only two years ago the official unemployment rate was still below 3 percent.

Even graver than the threat of unemployment is the threat to the country's social contract, especially the job security of lifetime employment. If the banks laid off large numbers of people, the social contract would shatter. The seriousness with which the Japanese view the social aspects of the crisis is shown by the lengths to which they will go to preserve a few jobs. They took the virtually unthinkable step of allowing (indeed, probably inviting) an American financial firm, Merrill Lynch, to take over the main branches of Yamaichi, Japan's fourth-largest bro-

kerage house, when it failed in 1997 simply because Merrill Lynch promised to keep on about a sixth of Yamaichi's
employees—a few thousand people. Only six weeks earlier senior officials in the Ministry of Finance, which oversees brokerage firms, had still loudly insisted that they
would never let a foreigner do domestic Japanese securities business.

The bank crisis undermines the structure of Japanese
business and society. It may dissolve Japan's most distinctive economic organization: the *keiretsu,* the cluster of
businesses around a major bank. Contrary to common belief in the West, the *keiretsu* does not primarily serve business purposes. Its first function is to act as the real board
of directors for the member companies, since the official
board of each individual company is just an internal management committee. The *keiretsu* quietly removes incompetent top management and checks out proposed
promotions into the top echelons of member companies.
But, above all, the *keiretsu* is a mutual support association.
The members of a component company collectively hold
enough of each other's shares to give the *keiretsu* effective
ownership control. It thus protects each member against
outsiders and hostile takeover bids. Moreover, it is the
ultimate guarantor of lifetime employment. If a *keiretsu*
member gets into such serious trouble that it has to lay
off people, the other *keiretsu* companies will provide jobs
for them. This lets the fellow *keiretsu* member cut costs
and still fulfill its commitment to permanent job security.

Can the *keiretsu* survive the financial crisis? The banks

at the core of the typical *keiretsu* have begun to sell off their holdings in the group in order to offset their losses. More *keiretsu* members are, in turn, selling off their shares in other *keiretsu* members to get cash to shore up their balance sheets. But, quite apart from the threat to lifetime employment and job security, what will replace the *keiretsu* as the organizing principle of the Japanese economy?

There are no answers to these questions. Thus, the only rational course for the Japanese bureaucracy may indeed be to have no policy. That delay will whittle the banking problem down to a manageable size is probably wishful thinking. But surely the West, especially the United States, can only hope that the procrastination strategy will work again. Social unrest in Japan would be a far more serious threat to U.S. political, strategic, and economic interests than anything that U.S. businesses or the U.S. economy could possibly gain through the actions, such as rapid deregulation of the financial sector, which Washington is now pressing on Tokyo.

It's the Society, Stupid

In the end, the most important key to understanding how the Japanese bureaucracy thinks, works, and behaves is understanding Japan's priorities. Americans assume that the economy takes primacy in political decisions, unless national security is seriously threatened. The Japanese—

and by no means the bureaucracy alone—accord primacy to society.

Again the United States is the exception and Japan more nearly the rule. In most developed countries other than the United States, the economy is considered a restraint on policies rather than their major, let alone sole, determinant. Ideology and, above all, the impact on society come first.

Even in the United States, the primacy of economics in public life and policy is fairly recent, dating no further back than World War II. Until then, the United States, too, tended to consider society first. Despite the Great Depression, the New Deal put social reform well ahead of economic recovery. America's voters overwhelmingly approved.

But while hardly uniquely Japanese, giving pride of place to society is more important to the Japanese than to most other developed countries, save perhaps France. To the outsider, Japan appears to have extraordinary social strength and cohesion. No other society in history has successfully met such extreme challenges and dislocations: say, the 180-degree turn forced on Japan by Commodore Perry's black ships in the 1860s, as a result of which the world's most isolated country, hermetically sealed for more than two centuries, opened itself to modernity overnight and became Westernized, or, equally traumatic, the radical social turnaround after its defeat in 1945 and the long years of foreign occupation thereafter. The Japanese, however, see their society as fragile. They know how

222

close to collapse and civil war their country came both times; hence the extreme importance, for instance, of lifetime employment as Japan's social glue.

Whether Japanese society is hardy or delicate is beside the point. What matters is that the Japanese take its primacy for granted. If Americans understood this, especially in dealing with a Japan in trouble, they might cling less to myths about the uselessness of the Japanese bureaucracy. Defending the bureaucrats is still heresy, of course, but heresy is often closer to the truth than conventional wisdom.

(1998)

14

On Civilizing the City

Civilizing the city will increasingly become top priority in all countries—and particularly in the developed countries such as the United States, the United Kingdom, and Japan. However, neither government nor business can provide the new communities that every major city in the world needs. That is the task of the nongovernmental, nonbusiness, nonprofit organization.

When I was born, a few years before the outbreak of World War I, less than 5 percent of the population—one out of every twenty human beings then living—lived and worked in a city. The city was still the exception, a small oasis in a rural universe. And even in the most highly industrialized and most highly urbanized countries, such as England or Belgium, the rural population was still a near majority.

Fifty years ago, at the end of World War II, a quarter of the American population was still rural—and in Japan, people living on the land still numbered three-fifths of the total. Today in both countries—and in every other developed country—the rural population has shrunk to less than 5 percent, and is still shrinking. And equally, in the developing world, it is the cities that are growing. Even in China and India, the two big countries that are still predominantly rural, the cities are growing while the rural population is at best maintaining itself. And in all developing countries people living on the land cannot wait to move into the city, even though there are no jobs for them there, and no housing.

The only precedent for this demographic transformation is what happened some ten thousand years ago, when our remote ancestors first settled on the land and became pastoralists and farmers. But that transformation took several thousand years. Ours has happened in less than a century. There is no modern precedent for it—and very few institutions and, alas, very few success stories. And the key to the survival and health of this new urban human society is the development of communities in the city.

Reality of Rural Life

In a rural society communities are a given for the individual. Community is a fact, whether family or religion, social class or caste. There is very little mobility in rural society, and what there is is mostly downward.

Rural society has been romanticized for millennia, especially in the West, where rural communities have usually been portrayed as idyllic. However, the community in the rural society is actually both compulsory and coercive.

One recent example. My family and I lived in rural Vermont only fifty years ago, in the late 1940s. At that time the most highly popularized character in the nation was the local telephone operator in the ads of the Bell Telephone Company. She, the ads told us every day, held her community together, served it, and was always available to help.

The reality was somewhat different. In rural Vermont, we then still had manual telephone exchanges. When you lifted the telephone, you did not get a dial tone. But at least—you hoped—you would get one of those wonderful, community-serving operators. But when finally, around 1947 or 1948, the dial telephone came to rural Vermont, there was universal celebration. Yes, the telephone operator was always there. But when, for instance, you called up to get Dr. Wilson, the pediatrician, because one of your children had a high fever, the operator would say, "You can't reach Dr. Wilson now; he is with his girl-friend." Or, "You don't need Dr. Wilson; your baby isn't that sick. Wait till tomorrow morning to see whether she still has a high temperature." Community was not only coercive; it was intrusive.

And this explains why, for millennia, the dream of rural people was to escape into the city. *Stadtluft macht frei* (city air frees) says an old German proverb dating back to the eleventh or twelfth century. The serf who managed to escape from the land and to be admitted into a city became a free man. He became a citizen. And so we, too, have an idyllic picture of the city—and it is as unrealistic as the idyllic picture of rural life.

For what made the city attractive also made it anarchic—the anonymity; the absence of coercive communities. The city was indeed the center of culture. It was where the artists and the scholars could work and flourish. Precisely because it had no community, it offered upward mobility. But beneath that thin layer of professionals, artists, and scholars, beneath the wealthy merchants and the highly skilled artisans in their craft guilds, there was moral and social anomie. There was prostitution and banditry and lawlessness. And also, city life meant exposure to disease and epidemics. Up to the last one hundred years or so, no city in the world maintained its own population levels; all depended on people moving in from the country. It was not until the nineteenth century, with modern water supply, modern sewerage, vaccination, and quarantine, that life expectancy in the city began to approach life expectancy in the country.

This was true of the Rome of the caesars, of Byzantine Constantinople, of the Florence of the Medici, of the Paris of Louis XIV (as portrayed so brilliantly in Dumas's *Three Musketeers*—the nineteenth century's greatest best-seller). But it was true, also, of Dickens's London. In the city was a brilliant "high culture." But it was a wafer-thin layer over a stinking swamp. And in no city, before 1880 or so, did a respectable woman dare go out alone at *any* time during the day. Nor was it safe for men to walk home at night.

The Need for Community

The city was attractive precisely because it offered freedom from the compulsory and coercive rural community. But it was destructive because it did not offer any community of its own.

And human beings need community. If there are no communities available for constructive ends, there will be destructive, murderous communities—the gangs of Victorian England, or the gangs that today threaten the very social fabric of the large American city (and increasingly of every large city in the world).

The first to point out that humans need community is one of the great classics of sociology, *Gemeinschaft und Gesellschaft* (Community and Society) by Ferdinand

Toennies, published in 1887. But the community that Toennies, over a century ago, still hoped to preserve—the organic community of traditional rural society—is gone, and gone for good. The task today, therefore, is to create urban communities—something that never existed before. Instead of the traditional communities of history, our communities need to be free and voluntary. But they also need to offer the individual in the city an opportunity to achieve, to contribute, to matter.

Since World War I—and certainly since the end of World War II—the majority in all countries, whether democracies or tyrannies, believed that government should and could supply the community needs of an urban society through "social programs." We now know that this was largely delusion. The social programs of the last fifty years have, by and large, not been successes. They certainly have not filled the vacuum created by the disappearance of traditional community. The needs were certainly there. And so has been the money (and in many countries in enormous quantity). But the results have been meager everywhere.

But it is equally clear that the private sector, business, cannot fill that need, either. I actually once thought that it could and would. More than fifty years ago, in my 1943 book, *The Future of Industrial Man,* I proposed what I then called the "self-governing plant community," the community within the new social organization, the large business enterprise. It has worked, but only in one country, Japan. And even there, it is by now clear, it is not the answer. In the first place, no business can really give security—the "lifetime employment" of the Japanese is rapidly proving to be a dangerous delusion. Above all, however, lifetime employment, and with it the "self-governing plant community," does not fit the reality of a knowledge society. There the private sector increasingly has become a way to make a living far more than a way to make a life. It will and should give material success and personal achievement. But the business enterprise is clearly what Toennies, 110 years ago, called a "society" rather than a "community."

The Only Answer

Only the social sector, that is, the nongovernmental, nonprofit organization, can create what we now need, communities for citizens—and especially for the highly educated knowledge workers who increasingly dominate developed societies. One reason for this is that only nonprofit organizations can provide the enormous diversity of communities we need—from churches to professional associations, from organizations taking care of the homeless to health clubs—if there are to be freely chosen communities for everyone. The nonprofit organizations also are the only ones that can satisfy the second need of the city, the need for effective citizenship for its people. Only social-sector institutions can provide opportunities to be a volunteer and thus enable individuals to have both a sphere in which they are in control and a sphere in which they make a difference.

The twentieth century, now coming to an end, has seen an explosive growth of both government and business—especially in the developed countries. What the dawning twenty-first century needs above all is equally explosive growth of the nonprofit social sector in building communities in the newly dominant social environment, the city.

(1998)

Part IV

THE NEXT SOCIETY

15

The Next Society

The New Economy may or may not materialize, but there is no doubt that the Next Society will be with us shortly. In the developed world, and probably in the emerging countries as well, this new society will be a good deal more important than the New Economy (if any). It will be quite different from the society of the late twentieth century, and also different from what most people expect. Much of it will be unprecedented. And most of it is already here, or is rapidly emerging.

In the developed countries, the dominant factor in the Next Society will be something to which most people are only just beginning to pay attention: the rapid growth in the older population and the rapid shrinking of the younger generation. Politicians everywhere still promise to save the existing pensions system, but they—and their constituents—know perfectly well that in another twenty-five years people will have to keep working until their mid-seventies, health permitting.

What has not yet sunk in is that a growing number of older people—say those over fifty—will not keep on working as traditional full-time nine-to-five employees, but will participate in the labor force in many new and different ways: as temporaries, as part-timers, as consultants, on special assignments, and so on. What used to be personnel departments and are now known as human-resources departments still assume that those who work for an organization are full-time employees. Employment laws and regulations are based on the same assumption. Within twenty or twenty-five years, however, perhaps as many as half the people who work for an organization will not be employed by it, certainly not full-time. This will be especially true for older people. New ways of working with people at arm's length will increasingly become the central managerial issue of employing organizations, and not just of businesses.

The shrinking of the younger population will cause an even greater upheaval, if only because nothing like this has happened since the dying centuries of the Roman empire. In every single developed country, but also in China and Brazil, the birthrate is now well below the replacement rate of 2.2 live births per woman of reproductive age. Politically, this means that immigration will become an important—and highly divisive—issue in all rich countries. It will cut across all traditional political alignments. Economically, the decline in the young population will change markets in fundamental ways. Growth in family formation has been the driving force of all domestic markets in the developed world, but the rate of family formation is certain to fall steadily unless bolstered by large-scale immigration of younger people. The homogeneous mass market that emerged in all rich countries after the Second World War has been youth-determined from the start. It will now become middle-age-determined, or perhaps more likely it will split into two: a middle-age-determined mass market and a much smaller youth-determined one. And because the supply of young people will shrink, creating new employment patterns to attract and hold the growing number of older people (especially older educated people) will become increasingly important.

Knowledge Is All

The Next Society will be a knowledge society. Knowledge will be its key resource, and knowledge workers will be the dominant group in its workforce. Its three main characteristics will be:

• Borderlessness, because knowledge travels even more effortlessly than money.

• Upward mobility, available to everyone through easily acquired formal education.
• The potential for failure as well as success. Anyone can acquire the "means of production," i.e., the knowledge required for the job, but not everyone can win.

Together, those three characteristics will make the knowledge society a highly competitive one, for organizations and individuals alike. Information technology, although only one of many new features of the Next Society, is already having one hugely important effect: It is allowing knowledge to spread near instantly, and making it accessible to everyone. Given the ease and speed at which information travels, every institution in the knowledge society—not only businesses, but also schools, universities, hospitals, and increasingly government agencies, too—has to be globally competitive, even though most organizations will continue to be local in their activities and in their markets. This is because the Internet will keep customers everywhere informed on what is available anywhere in the world, and at what price.

This new knowledge economy will rely heavily on knowledge workers. At present, this term is widely used to describe people with considerable theoretical knowledge and learning: doctors, lawyers, teachers, accountants, chemical engineers. But the most striking growth will be in "knowledge technologists": computer technicians, software designers, analysts in clinical labs, manufacturing technologists, paralegals. These people are as much manual workers as they are knowledge workers; in fact, they usually spend far more time working with their hands than with their brains. But their manual work is based on a substantial amount of theoretical knowledge that can be acquired only through formal education, not through an apprenticeship. They are not, as a rule, much better paid than traditional skilled workers, but they see themselves as "professionals." Just as unskilled manual workers in manufacturing were the dominant social and political force in the twentieth century, knowledge technologists are likely to become the dominant social—and perhaps also political—force over the next decades.

The New Protectionism

Structurally, too, the Next Society is already diverging from the society almost all of us still live in. The twentieth century saw the rapid decline of the sector that had dominated society for ten thousand years: agriculture. In volume terms, farm production now is at least four or five times what it was before the First World War. But in 1913 farm products accounted for 70 percent of world trade, whereas now their share is at most 17 percent. In the early years of the twentieth century, agriculture in most developed countries was the largest single contributor to GDP; now in rich countries its contribution has dwindled to the point of becoming marginal. And the farm population is down to a tiny proportion of the total.

Manufacturing has traveled a long way down the same road. Since the Second World War, manufacturing output in the developed world has probably tripled in volume, but inflation-adjusted manufacturing prices have fallen steadily, whereas the cost of prime knowledge products—health care and education—has tripled, again adjusted for inflation. The relative purchasing power of manufactured goods against knowledge products is now only one-fifth or one-sixth of what it was fifty years ago. Manufacturing employment in America has fallen from 35 percent of the workforce in the 1950s to less than half that now, without causing much social disruption. But it may be too much to hope for an equally easy transition in countries such as Japan or Germany, where blue-collar manufacturing workers still make up 25–30 percent of the labor force.

The decline of farming as a producer of wealth and of livelihoods has allowed farm protectionism to spread to a degree that would have been unthinkable before the Second World War. In the same way, the decline of manufacturing will trigger an explosion of manufacturing protectionism—even as lip service continues to be paid to free trade. This protectionism may not necessarily take the form of traditional tariffs, but of subsidies, quotas, and regulations of all kinds. Even more likely, regional blocks will emerge that trade freely internally but are highly protectionist externally. The European Union, NAFTA, and Mercosur already point in that direction.

The Future of the Corporation

Statistically, multinational companies play much the same part in the world economy as they did in 1913. But they have become very different animals. Multinationals in 1913 were domestic firms with subsidiaries abroad, each of them self-contained, in charge of a politically defined territory, and highly autonomous. Multinationals now tend to be organized globally along product or service lines. But like the multinationals of 1913, they are held together and controlled by ownership. By contrast, the multinationals of 2025 are likely to be held together and controlled by strategy. There will still be ownership, of course. But alliances, joint ventures, minority stakes, know-how agreements, and contracts will increasingly be the building blocks of a confederation. This kind of organization will need a new kind of top management.

In most countries, and even in a good many large and complex companies, top management is still seen as an extension of operating management. Tomorrow's top management, however, is likely to be a distinct and separate organ: It will stand for the company. One of the most important jobs ahead for the top management of the big company of tomorrow, and especially of the multinational, will be to balance the conflicting demands on business being made by the need for both short-term and long-term results, and by the corporation's various constituencies: customers, shareholders (especially institutional investors and pension funds), knowledge employees, and communities.

Against that background, this survey will seek to answer two questions: What can and should managements do now to be ready for the Next Society? And what other big changes may lie ahead of which we are as yet unaware?

◆ *The New Demographics*

By 2030, people over sixty-five in Germany, the world's third-largest economy, will account for almost half the adult population, compared with one-fifth now. And unless the country's birthrate recovers from its present low of 1.3 per woman, over the same period its population of under-thirty-fives will shrink about twice as fast as the older population will grow. The net result will be that the total population, now 82 million, will decline to 70–73 million. The number of people of working age will fall by a full quarter, from 40 million today to 30 million.

The German demographics are far from exceptional. In Japan, the world's second-largest economy, the population will peak in 2005, at around 125 million. By 2050, according to the more pessimistic government forecasts, the population will have shrunk to around 95 million. Long before that, around 2030, the share of the over-sixty-fives in the adult population will have grown to about half. And the birthrate in Japan, as in Germany, is down to 1.3 per woman.

The figures are pretty much the same for most other developed countries—Italy, France, Spain, Portugal, the Netherlands, Sweden—and for a good many emerging ones, especially China. In some regions, such as central Italy, southern France, or southern Spain, birthrates are even lower than in Germany or Japan.

Life expectancy—and with it the number of older people—has been going up steadily for three hundred years. But the decline in the number of young people is something new. The only developed country that has so far avoided this fate is America. But even there the birthrate is well below replacement level, and the proportion of older people in the adult population will rise steeply in the next thirty years.

All this means that winning the support of older people will become a political imperative in every developed country. Pensions have already become a regular election issue. There is also a growing debate about the desirability of immigration to maintain population and workforce. Together these two issues are transforming the political landscape in every developed country.

By 2030 at the latest, the age at which full retirement benefits start will have risen to the midseventies in all developed countries, and benefits for healthy pensioners will be substantially lower than they are today. Indeed, fixed retirement ages for people in reasonable physical and mental condition may have been abolished to prevent the pensions burden on the working population from becoming unbearable. Already young and middle-aged people at work suspect that there will not be enough pension money to go round when they themselves reach traditional retirement age. But politicians everywhere continue to pretend that they can save the current pensions system.

Needed but Unwanted

Immigration is certain to be an even hotter issue. The respected DIW research institute in Berlin estimates that by 2020 Germany will have to import 1 million immigrants of working age each year simply to maintain its workforce. Other rich European countries are in the same boat. And in Japan there is talk of admitting five hundred thousand Koreans each year—and sending them home five years later. For all big countries but America, immigration on such a scale is unprecedented.

The political implications are already being felt. In 1999 fellow Europeans were shocked by the electoral success in Austria of a xenophobic right-wing party whose main plank is "no immigration." Similar movements are growing in Flemish-speaking Belgium, in traditionally liberal Denmark, and in northern Italy. Even in America, immigration is upsetting long-established political alignments. American trade unions' opposition to large-scale immigration has put them in the antiglobalization camp that organized violent protests during the Seattle meeting of the World Trade Organization in 1999. A future Democratic candidate for the American presidency may have to choose between getting the union vote by opposing immigration, or getting the vote of Latinos and other newcomers by supporting it. Equally, a future Republican candidate may have to choose between the support of business, which is clamoring for workers, and the vote of a white middle class that increasingly opposes immigration.

Even so, America's experience of immigration should give it a lead in the developed world for several decades to come. Since the 1970s it has been admitting large numbers of immigrants, either legally or illegally. Most immigrants are young, and the birthrates of first-generation immigrant women tend to be higher than those of their adopted country. This means that for the next thirty or forty years America's population will continue to grow, albeit slowly, whereas in some other developed countries it will fall.

A Country of Immigrants

But it is not numbers alone that will give America an advantage. Even more important, the country is culturally attuned to immigration and long ago learned to integrate immigrants into its society and economy. In fact, recent immigrants, whether Hispanics or Asians, may be integrating faster than ever. One-third of all recent Hispanic immigrants, for instance, are reported to be marrying non-Hispanics and nonimmigrants. The one big obstacle to the full integration of recent immigrants in America is the poor performance of American public schools.

Among developed countries, only Australia and Canada have a tradition of immigration similar to America's. Japan has resolutely kept foreigners out, except for a spate of Korean immigrants in the 1920s and 1930s, whose descendants are still being discriminated against. The mass migrations of the nineteenth century were either into empty, unsettled spaces (such as the United States, Canada, Australia, Brazil), or from farm to city within the same country. By contrast, immigration in the twenty-first century is by foreigners—in nationality, language, culture, and religion—who move into settled countries. European countries have so far been less than successful at integrating such foreigners.

The biggest effect of the demographic changes may be to split hitherto homogeneous societies and markets. Until the 1920s or 1930s, every country had a diversity of cultures and markets. They were sharply differentiated by class, occupation, and residence, e.g., "the farm market" or "the carriage trade," both of which disappeared sometime between 1920 and 1940. Yet since the Second World War, all developed countries have had only one mass culture and one mass market. Now that demographic forces in all the developed countries are pulling in opposite directions, will that homogeneity survive?

The markets of the developed world have been dominated by the values, habits, and preferences of the young population. Some of the most successful and most profitable businesses of the past half-century, such as Coca-Cola and Procter & Gamble in America, Unilever in Britain, and Henckel in Germany, owe their prosperity in large measure to the growth of the young population and to the high rate of family formation between 1950 and 2000. The same is true of the car industry over that period.

The End of the Single Market

Now there are signs that the market is splitting. In financial services, perhaps America's fastest-growing industry over the past twenty-five years, it has split already. The bubble market of the 1990s, with its frantic day-trading in high-tech stocks, belonged mainly to the under-forty-fives. But the customers in the markets for investments, such as mutual funds or deferred annuities, tend to be over fifty, and that market has also been growing apace. The fastest-growing industry in any developed country may turn out to be the continuing education of already well-educated adults, which is based on values that are all but incompatible with those of the youth culture.

But it is also conceivable that some youth markets will become exceedingly lucrative. In the coastal cities of China, where the government was able to enforce its one-child policy, middle-class families are now reported to spend more on their one child than earlier middle-class families spent on their four or five children together. This seems to be true in Japan, too. Many American middle-class families are spending heavily on the education of their single child, mainly by moving into expensive suburban neighborhoods with good schools. But this new luxury youth market is quite different from the homogeneous mass market of the past fifty years. That mass market is rapidly weakening because of the decline in the numbers of young people reaching adulthood.

In future there will almost certainly be two distinct workforces, broadly made up of the under-fifties and the over-fifties respectively. These two workforces are likely to differ markedly in their needs and behavior, and in the jobs they do. The younger group will need a steady income from a permanent job, or at least a succession of full-time jobs. The rapidly growing older group will have much more choice and will be able to combine traditional jobs, nonconventional jobs, and leisure in whatever proportion suits them best.

The split into two workforces is likely to start with female knowledge technologists. A nurse, a computer technologist, or a paralegal can take fifteen years out to look after her children and then return to full-time work. Women, who now outnumber men in American higher education, increasingly look for work in the new knowledge technologies. Such jobs are the first in human history to be well adapted to the special needs of women as childbearers, and to their increasing longevity. That longevity is one of the reasons for the split in the job market. A fifty-year working life—unprecedented in human history—is simply too long for one kind of work.

The second reason for the split is a shrinking life expectancy for businesses and organizations of all kinds. In the past, employing organizations have outlived employees. In future, employees, and especially knowledge workers, will increasingly outlive even successful organizations. Few businesses, or even government agencies or programs, last for more than thirty years. Historically, the working life span of most employees has been less than thirty years because most manual workers simply wore out. But knowledge workers who enter the labor force in their twenties are likely to be still in good physical and mental shape fifty years later.

Second career and *second half of one's life* have already become buzzwords in America. Increasingly, employees there take early retirement as soon as their pension and social security rights are guaranteed for the time when they reach traditional retirement age; but they do not stop working. Instead, their "second career" often takes an unconventional form. They may work freelance (and often forget to tell the taxman about their work, thus boosting their net income) or part-time or as "temporaries" or for an outsourcing contractor or as contractors themselves. Such "early retirement to keep on working" is particularly common among knowledge workers, who are still a minority among people now reaching fifty or fifty-five, but will become the largest single group of older people in America from about 2030.

Beware Demographic Changes

Population predictions for the next twenty years can be made with some certainty because almost everybody who will be in the workforce in 2020 is already alive. But, as American experience in the past couple of decades has shown, demographic trends can change quite suddenly and unpredictably, with fairly immediate effects. The American baby boom of the late 1940s, for instance, triggered the housing boom of the 1950s.

In the mid-1920s America had its first "baby bust." Between 1925 and 1935 the birthrate declined by almost half, dipping below the replacement rate of 2.2 live births per woman. In the late 1930s, President Roosevelt's Commission on American Population (consisting of the country's most eminent demographers and statisticians) confidently predicted that America's population would peak in 1945 and would then start declining. But an exploding birthrate in the late 1940s proved it wrong. Within ten years, the number of live births per woman doubled from 1.8 to 3.6. Between 1947 and 1957, America experienced an astonishing "baby boom." The number of babies born rose from 2.5 million to 4.1 million.

Then, in 1960–61, the opposite happened. Instead of

the expected second-wave baby boom as the first boomers reached adulthood, there was a big bust. Between 1961 and 1975, the birthrate fell from 3.7 to 1.8. The number of babies born went down from 4.3 million in 1960 to 3.1 million in 1975. The next surprise was the "baby boom echo" in the late 1980s and early 1990s. The number of live births went up quite sharply, surpassing even the numbers of the first baby boom's peak years. With the benefit of hindsight, it is now clear that this echo was triggered by large-scale immigration into America, beginning in the early 1970s. When the girls born to these early immigrants started having children of their own in the late 1980s, their birthrates were still closer to those of their parents' country of origin than to those of their adopted country. Fully one-fifth of all children of school age in California in the first decade of this century have at least one foreign-born parent.

But nobody knows what caused the two baby busts, or the baby boom of the 1940s. Both busts occurred when the economy was doing well, which in theory should have encouraged people to have lots of children. And the baby boom should never have happened, because historically birthrates have always gone down after a big war. The truth is that we simply do not understand what determines birthrates in modern societies. So demographics will not only be the most important factor in the Next Society, it will also be the least predictable and least controllable one.

♦ *The New Workforce*

A century ago, the overwhelming majority of people in developed countries worked with their hands: on farms, in domestic service, in small craft shops, and (at that time still a small minority) in factories. Fifty years later, the proportion of manual workers in the American labor force had dropped to around half, but factory workers had become the largest single section of the workforce, making up 35 percent of the total. Now, another fifty years later, fewer than a quarter of American workers make their living from manual jobs. Factory workers still account for the majority of the manual workers, but their share of the total workforce is down to around 15 percent—more or less back to what it had been one hundred years earlier.

Of all the big developed countries, America now has the smallest proportion of factory workers in its labor force. Britain is not far behind. In Japan and Germany, their share is still around a quarter, but it is shrinking steadily. To some extent this is a matter of definition. Data-processing employees of a manufacturing firm, such as the Ford Motor Company, are counted as employed in manufacturing, but when Ford outsources its data processing, the same people doing exactly the same work are instantly redefined as service workers. However, too much should not be made of this. Many studies in manufacturing businesses have shown that the decline in the number of people who actually work in the plant is roughly the same as the shrinkage reported in the national figures.

Before the First World War there was not even a word for people who made their living other than by manual work. The term *service worker* was coined around 1920, but it has turned out to be rather misleading. These days, fewer than half of all nonmanual workers are actually service workers. The only fast-growing group in the workforce, in America and in every other developed country, is "knowledge workers"—people whose jobs require formal and advanced schooling. They now account for a full third of the American workforce, outnumbering factory workers by two to one. In another twenty years or so, they are likely to make up close to two-fifths of the workforce of all rich countries.

The terms *knowledge industries, knowledge work,* and *knowledge worker* are only forty years old. They were coined around 1960, simultaneously but independently; the first by a Princeton economist, Fritz Machlup, the second and third by this writer. Now everyone uses them, but as yet hardly anyone understands their implications for human values and human behavior, for managing people and making them productive, for economics and for politics. What is already clear, however, is that the emerging knowledge society and knowledge economy will be radically different from the society and economy of the late twentieth century, in the following ways.

First, the knowledge workers, collectively, are the new

capitalists. Knowledge has become the key resource, and the only scarce one. This means that knowledge workers collectively own the means of production. But as a group, they are also capitalists in the old sense: Through their stakes in pension funds and mutual funds, they have become majority shareholders and owners of many large businesses in the knowledge society.

Effective knowledge is specialized. That means knowledge workers need access to an organization—a collective that brings together an array of knowledge workers and applies their specialisms to a common end product. The most gifted mathematics teacher in a secondary school is effective only as a member of the faculty. The most brilliant consultant on product development is effective only if there is an organized and competent business to convert her advice into action. The greatest software designer needs a hardware producer. But in turn the high school needs the mathematics teacher, the business needs the expert on product development, and the PC manufacturer needs the software programmer. Knowledge workers therefore see themselves as equal to those who retain their services, as "professionals" rather than as "employees." The knowledge society is a society of seniors and juniors rather than of bosses and subordinates.

His and Hers

All this has important implications for the role of women in the labor force. Historically women's participation in the world of work has always equaled men's. The lady of leisure sitting in her parlor was the rarest of exceptions even in a wealthy nineteenth-century society. A farm, a craftsman's business, or a small shop had to be run by a couple to be viable. As late as the beginning of the twentieth century, a doctor could not start a practice until he had got married; he needed a wife to make appointments, open the door, take patients' histories, and send out the bills.

But although women have always worked, since time immemorial the jobs they have done have been different from men's. There was men's work and there was women's work. Countless women in the Bible go to the well to fetch water, but not one man. There never was a male spinster. Knowledge work, on the other hand, is "unisex," not because of feminist pressure but because it can be done equally well by both sexes. Still, the first modern knowledge jobs were designed for only one or the other sex. Teaching as a profession was invented in 1794, the year the École Normale was founded in Paris, and was seen strictly as a man's job. Sixty years later, during the Crimean War of 1853–56, Florence Nightingale founded the second new knowledge profession, nursing. This was considered as exclusively women's work. But by 1850 teaching everywhere had become unisex, and in 2000 two-fifths of America's students at nursing schools were men.

There were no women doctors in Europe until the 1890s. But one of the earliest European women to get a medical doctorate, the great Italian educator Maria Montessori, reportedly said: "I am not a woman doctor; I am a doctor who happens to be a woman." The same logic applies to all knowledge work. Knowledge workers, whatever their sex, are professionals, applying the same knowledge, doing the same work, governed by the same standards, and judged by the same results.

High-knowledge workers such as doctors, lawyers, scientists, clerics, and teachers have been around for a long time, although their number has increased exponentially in the past hundred years. The largest group of knowledge workers, however, barely existed until the start of the twentieth century and took off only after the Second World War. They are knowledge technologists—people who do much of their work with their hands (and to that extent are the successors to skilled workers), but whose pay is determined by the knowledge between their ears, acquired in formal education rather than through apprenticeship. They include X-ray technicians, physiotherapists, ultrasound specialists, psychiatric caseworkers, dental technicians, and scores of others. In the past thirty years, medical technologists have been the fastest-growing segment of the labor force in America, and probably in Britain as well.

In the next twenty or thirty years the number of knowledge technologists in computers, manufacturing, and education is likely to grow even faster. Office technologists such as paralegals are also proliferating. And it is no accident that yesterday's "secretary" is rapidly turning into an "assistant," having become the manager of the boss's office and of his work. Within two or three decades, knowledge technologists will become the dominant group in the workforce in all developed countries, occupying the same position that unionized factory workers held at the peak of their power in the 1950s and 1960s.

The most important thing about these knowledge workers is that they do not identify themselves as "workers" but as "professionals." Many of them spend a good deal of their time doing largely unskilled work, e.g., straightening out patients' beds, answering the telephone, or filing. However, what identifies them in their own and in the public's mind is the part of their job that involves putting their formal knowledge to work. That makes them full-fledged knowledge workers.

Such workers have two main needs: formal education that enables them to enter knowledge work in the first place, and continuing education throughout their working lives to keep their knowledge up-to-date. For the old high-knowledge professionals such as doctors, clerics, and lawyers, formal education has been available for many centuries. But for knowledge technologists, only a few countries so far provide systematic and organized preparation. Over the next few decades, educational institutions to prepare knowledge technologists will grow rapidly in all developed and emerging countries, just as new institutions to meet new requirements have always appeared in the past. What is different this time is the need for the continuing education of already well-trained and highly knowledgeable adults. Schooling traditionally stopped when work began. In the knowledge society it never stops.

Knowledge is unlike traditional skills, which change very slowly. A museum near Barcelona in Spain contains a vast number of the hand tools used by the skilled craftsmen of the late Roman empire that any craftsman today would instantly recognize, because they are very similar to the tools still in use. For the purposes of skill training, therefore, it was reasonable to assume that whatever had been learned by age seventeen or eighteen would last for a lifetime.

Conversely, knowledge rapidly becomes obsolete, and knowledge workers regularly have to go back to school. Continuing education of already highly educated adults will therefore become a big growth area in the Next Society. But most of it will be delivered in nontraditional ways, ranging from weekend seminars to on-line training programs, and in any number of places, from a traditional university to the student's home. The Information Revolution, which is expected to have an enormous impact on education and on traditional schools and universities, will probably have an even greater effect on the continuing education of knowledge workers.

Knowledge workers of all kinds tend to identify themselves with their knowledge. They introduce themselves by saying "I am an anthropologist" or "I am a physiotherapist." They may be proud of the organization they work for, be it a company, a university, or a government agency, but they "work at the organization"; they do not "belong to it." Most of them probably feel that they have more in common with someone who practices the same specialism in another institution than with their colleagues at their own institution who work in a different knowledge area.

Although the emergence of knowledge as an important resource increasingly means specialization, knowledge workers are highly mobile within their specialism. They think nothing of moving from one university, one company, or one country to another, as long as they stay within the same field of knowledge. There is a lot of talk about trying to restore knowledge workers' loyalty to their employing organization, but such efforts will get nowhere. Knowledge workers may have an attachment to an organization and feel comfortable with it, but their primary allegiance is likely to be to their specialized branch of knowledge.

Knowledge is nonhierarchical. Either it is relevant in a given situation, or it is not. An open-heart surgeon may be much better paid than, say, a speech therapist and enjoy a much higher social status, yet if a particular situation requires the rehabilitation of a stroke victim, then in that instance the speech therapist's knowledge is greatly superior to that of the surgeon. This is why knowledge workers of all kinds see themselves not as subordinates but as professionals and expect to be treated as such.

Money is as important to knowledge workers as to anybody else, but they do not accept it as the ultimate yardstick, nor do they consider money as a substitute for professional performance and achievement. In sharp contrast to yesterday's workers, to whom a job was first of all a living, most knowledge workers see their job as a life.

Ever Upward

The knowledge society is the first human society where upward mobility is potentially unlimited. Knowledge differs from all other means of production in that it cannot be inherited or bequeathed. It has to be acquired anew by every individual, and everyone starts out with the same total ignorance.

Knowledge has to be put in a form in which it can be taught, which means it has to become public. It is always universally accessible or quickly becomes so. All this makes the knowledge society a highly mobile one. Anyone can acquire any knowledge at a school, through a codified learning process, rather than by serving as an apprentice to a master.

Until 1850 or perhaps even 1900, there was little mobility in any society. The Indian caste system, in which birth determines not only an individual's status in society but his occupation as well, was only an extreme case. In most other societies, too, if the father was a peasant, the son was a peasant, and the daughters married peasants. By and large, the only mobility was downward, caused by war or disease, personal misfortune, or bad habits such as drinking or gambling.

Even in America, the land of unlimited opportunities, there was far less upward mobility than is commonly believed. The great majority of professionals and managers in America in the first half of the twentieth century were still the children of professionals and managers rather than the children of farmers, small shopkeepers, or factory workers. What distinguished America was not the amount of upward mobility but, in sharp contrast to most European countries, the way it was welcomed, encouraged, and cherished.

The knowledge society takes this approval of upward mobility much further: it considers every impediment to such mobility a form of discrimination. This implies that everybody is now expected to be a "success"—an idea that would have seemed ludicrous to earlier generations. Naturally, only a tiny number of people can be outstanding successes; but a very large number are expected to be adequately successful.

In 1958 John Kenneth Galbraith first wrote about "the affluent society." This was not a society with many more rich people, or in which the rich were richer, but one in which the majority could feel financially secure. In the knowledge society, a large number of people, perhaps even a majority, have something even more important than financial security: social standing or "social affluence."

261

The Price of Success

The upward mobility of the knowledge society, however, comes at a high price: the psychological pressures and emotional traumas of the rat race. There can be winners only if there are losers. This was not true of earlier societies. The son of the landless laborer who became a landless laborer himself was not a failure. In the knowledge society, however, he is not only a personal failure but a failure of society as well.

Japanese youngsters suffer sleep deprivation because they spend their evenings at a crammer to help them pass their exams. Otherwise they will not get into the prestige university of their choice, and thus into a good job. These pressures create hostility to learning. They also threaten to undermine Japan's prized economic equality and turn the country into a plutocracy, because only well-off parents can afford the prohibitive cost of preparing their youngsters for university. Other countries, such as America, Britain, and France, are also allowing their schools to become viciously competitive. That this has happened over such a short time—no more than thirty or forty years—indicates how much the fear of failure has already permeated the knowledge society.

Given this competitive struggle, a growing number of highly successful knowledge workers of both sexes— business managers, university teachers, museum directors, doctors—"plateau" in their forties. They know they have achieved all they will achieve. If their work is all they have, they are in trouble. Knowledge workers therefore need to develop, preferably while they are still young, a noncompetitive life and community of their own, and some serious outside interest—be it working as a volunteer in the community, playing in a local orchestra, or taking an active part in a small town's local government. This outside interest will give them the opportunity for personal contribution and achievement.

◆ *The Manufacturing Paradox*

In the closing years of the twentieth century, the world price of the steel industry's biggest single product—hot-rolled coil, the steel for car bodies—plunged from $460 to $260 a ton. Yet these were boom years in America and prosperous times in most of continental Europe, with automobile production setting records. The steel industry's experience is typical of manufacturing as a whole. Between 1960 and 1999, both manufacturing's share in America's GDP and its share of total employment roughly halved, to around 15 percent. Yet in the same forty years manufacturing's physical output doubled or tripled. In 1960, manufacturing was the center of the American economy, and of the economies of all other developed countries. By 2000, as a contributor to GDP it was easily outranked by the financial sector.

The relative purchasing power of manufactured goods (what economists call the terms of trade) has fallen by three-quarters in the past forty years. Whereas manufacturing prices, adjusted for inflation, are down by 40 percent, the prices of the two main knowledge products, health care and education, have risen about three times as fast as inflation. In 2000, therefore, it took five times as many units of manufactured goods to buy the main knowledge products as it had done forty years earlier.

The purchasing power of workers in manufacturing has also gone down, although by much less than that of their products. Their productivity has risen so sharply that most of their real income has been preserved. Forty years ago, labor costs in manufacturing typically accounted for around 30 percent of total manufacturing costs; now they are generally down to 12–15 percent. Even in cars, still the most labor-intensive of the engineering industries, labor costs in the most advanced plants are no higher than 20 percent. Manufacturing workers, especially in America, have ceased to be the backbone of the consumer market. At the height of the crisis in America's "rust belt," when employment in the big manufacturing centers was ruthlessly slashed, national sales of consumer goods barely budged.

What has changed manufacturing, and sharply pushed up productivity, are new concepts. Information and automation are less important than new theories of manufacturing, which are an advance comparable to the arrival of mass production eighty years ago. Indeed, some of these theories, such as Toyota's "lean manufacturing," do away with robots, computers, and automation. One highly publicized example involves replacing one of Toyota's automated and computerized paint-drying lines by half a dozen hairdryers bought in a supermarket.

Manufacturing is following exactly the same path that farming trod earlier. Beginning in 1920, and accelerating after the Second World War, farm production shot up in all developed countries. Before the First World War, many Western European countries had to import farm products. Now there is only one net farm importer left: Japan. Every single European country now has large and increasingly unsalable farm surpluses. In quantitative terms, farm production in most developed countries today is probably at least four times what it was in 1920 and three times what it was in 1950 (except in Japan). But whereas at the beginning of the twentieth century farmers made up the largest single group in the working population in most developed countries, now they account for no more than 3 percent in any developed country. And whereas at the beginning of the twentieth century agriculture was the largest single contributor to national income in most developed countries, in 2000 in America it contributed less than 2 percent to GDP.

Manufacturing is unlikely to expand its output in volume terms as much as agriculture did, or to shrink as much as a producer of wealth and of jobs. But the most believable forecast for 2020 suggests that manufacturing output in the developed countries will at least double, while manufacturing employment will shrink to 10–12 percent of the total workforce.

In America, the transition has largely been accomplished already, and with a minimum of dislocation. The only hard-hit group have been African-Americans, to whom the growth in manufacturing jobs after the Second World War offered quick economic advancement, and whose jobs have now sharply fallen. But by and large, even in places that relied heavily on a few large manufacturing plants, unemployment remained high only for a short time. Even the political impact in America has been minimal.

But will other industrial countries have an equally easy passage? In Britain, manufacturing employment has already fallen quite sharply without causing any unrest, although it seems to have produced social and psychological problems. But what will happen in countries such as Germany or France, where labor markets remain rigid and where, until very recently, there has been little upward mobility through education? These countries already have substantial and seemingly intractable unemployment, e.g., in Germany's Ruhr and in France's old industrial area around Lille. They may face a painful transition period with severe social upheavals.

The biggest question mark is over Japan. To be sure, it has no working-class culture, and it has long appreciated the value of education as an instrument of upward mobility. But Japan's social stability is based on employment security, especially for blue-collar workers in big manufacturing industry, and that is eroding fast. Yet before employment security was introduced for blue-collar workers in the 1950s, Japan had been a country of extreme labor turbulence. Manufacturing's share of total employment is still higher than in almost any other developed country— around a quarter of the total—and Japan has practically no labor market and little labor mobility.

Psychologically, too, the country is least prepared for the decline in manufacturing. After all, it has owed its rise to great-economic-power status in the second half of the twentieth century to becoming the world's manufacturing virtuoso. One should never underrate the Japanese. Throughout their history they have shown unparalleled ability to face up to reality and to change practically overnight. But the decline in manufacturing as the key to economic success confronts Japan with one of the biggest challenges ever.

The decline of manufacturing as a producer of wealth and jobs changes the world's economic, social, and political landscape. It makes "economic miracles" increasingly difficult for developing countries to achieve. The economic miracles of the second half of the twentieth century—Japan, South Korea, Taiwan, Hong Kong, Singapore—were based on exports to the world's rich countries of manufactured goods that were produced with developed-country technology and productivity but with emerging-country labor costs. This will no longer work.

One way to generate economic development may be to integrate the economy of an emerging country into a developed region—which is what Vicente Fox, the new Mexican president, envisages with his proposal for total integration of "North America," i.e., the United States, Canada, and Mexico. Economically this makes a lot of sense, but politically it is almost unthinkable. The alternative—which is being pursued by China—is to try to achieve economic growth by building up a developing country's domestic market. India, Brazil, and Mexico also have large enough populations to make home-market-based economic development feasible, at least in theory. But will smaller countries, such as Paraguay or Thailand, be allowed to export to the large markets of emerging countries such as Brazil?

The decline in manufacturing as a creator of wealth and jobs will inevitably bring about a new protectionism, once again echoing what happened earlier in agriculture. For every 1 percent by which agricultural prices and employment have fallen in the twentieth century, agricultural subsidies and protection in every single developed country, including America, have gone up by at least 1 percent, often more. And the fewer farm voters there are, the more important the "farm vote" has become. As numbers have shrunk, farmers have become a unified special-interest group that carries disproportionate clout in all rich countries.

Protectionism in manufacturing is already in evidence, although it tends to take the form of subsidies instead of traditional tariffs. The new regional economic blocks, such as the European Union, NAFTA, or Mercosur, do create large regional markets with lower internal barriers, but they protect them with higher barriers against producers outside the region. And nontariff barriers of all kinds are steadily growing. In the same week in which the 40 percent decline in sheet-steel prices was announced in the American press, the American government banned sheet-steel imports as "dumping." And no matter how laudable their aims, the developed countries' insistence on fair labor laws and adequate environmental rules for manufacturers in the developing world acts as a mighty barrier to imports from these countries.

Smaller Numbers, Bigger Clout

Politically, too, manufacturing is becoming more influential the fewer manufacturing workers there are, especially in America. In last year's presidential election the labor vote was more important than it had been forty or fifty years earlier, precisely because the number of trade-union members has become so much smaller as a percentage of the voting population. Feeling endangered, they have closed ranks. A few decades ago, a substantial minority of American union members voted Republican, but in last year's election more than 90 percent of union members are thought to have voted Democrat (though their candidate still lost).

For over one hundred years, America's trade unions had been strong supporters of free trade, at least in their rhetoric, but in the past few years they have become staunchly protectionist and declared enemies of "globalization." No matter that the real threat to manufacturing jobs is not competition from abroad, but the rapid decline of manufacturing as a creator of work: It is simply incomprehensible that manufacturing production can go up while manufacturing jobs go down, and not only to trade unionists but also to politicians, journalists, economists, and the public at large. Most people continue to believe that when manufacturing jobs decline, the country's manufacturing base is threatened and has to be protected. They have great difficulty in accepting that, for the first time in history, society and economy are no longer dominated by manual work, and a country can feed, house, and clothe itself with only a small minority of its population engaged in such work.

The new protectionism is driven as much by nostalgia and deep-seated emotion as by economic self-interest and political power. Yet it will achieve nothing, because "protecting" aging industries does not work. That is the clear lesson of seventy years of farm subsidies. The old crops—corn (maize), wheat, cotton—into which America has pumped countless billions since the 1930s—have all done poorly, whereas unprotected and unsubsidized new crops—such as soybeans—have flourished. The lesson is clear: Policies that pay old industries to hold on to redundant people can only do harm. Whatever money is being spent should instead go to subsidizing the incomes of older laid-off workers and to retraining and redeploying younger ones.

◆ *Will the Corporation Survive?*

For most of the time since the corporation was invented around 1870, the following five basic points have been assumed to apply:

1. The corporation is the "master," the employee is the "servant." Because the corporation owns the means of production without which the employee could not make a living, the employee needs the corporation more than the corporation needs the employee.

2. The great majority of employees work full-time for the corporation. The pay they get for the job is their only income and provides their livelihood.

3. The most efficient way to produce anything is to bring together under one management as many as possible of the activities needed to turn out the product.

The theory underlying this was not developed until after the Second World War, by Ronald Coase, an Anglo-American economist, who argued that bringing together activities into one company lowers "transactional costs," and especially the cost of communications (for which the-

271

ory he received the 1991 Nobel Prize in economics). But the concept itself was discovered and put into practice seventy or eighty years earlier by John D. Rockefeller. He saw that to put exploration, production, transport, refining, and selling into one corporate structure resulted in the most efficient and lowest-cost petroleum operation. On this insight he built the Standard Oil Trust, probably the most profitable large enterprise in business history. The concept was carried to an extreme by Henry Ford in the early 1920s. The Ford Motor Company not only produced all parts of the automobile and assembled it, but it also made its own steel, its own glass, and its own tires. It owned the plantations in the Amazon that grew the rubber trees, owned and ran the railroad that carried supplies to the plant and carried the finished cars from it, and planned eventually to sell and service Ford cars, too (though it never did).

4. Suppliers and especially manufacturers have market power because they have information about a product or a service that the customer does not and cannot have, and does not need if he can trust the brand. This explains the profitability of brands.

5. To any one particular technology pertains one and only one industry, and conversely, to any one particular industry pertains one and only one technology.

This means that all technology needed to make steel is peculiar to the steel industry; and conversely, that whatever technology is being used to make steel comes out of the steel industry itself. The same applies to the paper industry, to agriculture, or to banking and commerce.

On this assumption were founded the industrial research labs, beginning with Siemens's, started in Germany in 1869, and ending with IBM's, the last of the great traditional labs, founded in America in 1952. Each of them concentrated on the technology needed for a single industry, and each assumed that its discoveries would be applied in that industry.

Similarly, everybody took it for granted that every product or service had a specific application, and that for every application there was a specific product or material. So beer and milk were sold only in glass bottles; car bodies were made only from steel; working capital for a business was supplied by a commercial bank through a commercial loan; and so on. Competition therefore took place mainly within an industry. By and large, it was obvious what the business of a given company was and what its markets were.

Everything in Its Place

Every one of these assumptions remained valid for a whole century, but from 1970 onward every one of them has been turned upside down. The list now reads as follows:

1. The means of production is knowledge, which is owned by knowledge workers and is highly portable. This

273

applies equally to high-knowledge workers such as research scientists and to knowledge technologists such as physiotherapists, computer technicians, and paralegals. Knowledge workers provide "capital" just as much as does the provider of money. The two are dependent on each other. This makes the knowledge worker an equal— an associate or a partner.

2. Many employees, perhaps a majority, will still have full-time jobs with a salary that provides their only or main income. But a growing number of people who work for an organization will not be full-time employees but part-timers, temporaries, consultants, or contractors. Even of those who do have a full-time job, a large and growing number may not be employees of the organization for which they work, but employees of, e.g., an outsourcing contractor.

3. There always were limits to the importance of transactional costs. Henry Ford's all-inclusive Ford Motor Company proved unmanageable and became a disaster. But now the traditional axiom that an enterprise should aim for maximum integration has become almost entirely invalidated. One reason is that the knowledge needed for any activity has become highly specialized. It is therefore increasingly expensive, and also increasingly difficult, to maintain enough critical mass for every major task within an enterprise. And because knowledge rapidly deteriorates unless it is used constantly, maintaining within an organization an activity that is used only intermittently guarantees incompetence.

The second reason why maximum integration is no longer needed is that communications costs have come down so fast as to become insignificant. This decline began well before the Information Revolution. Perhaps its biggest cause has been the growth and spread of business literacy. When Rockefeller built his Standard Oil Trust, he had great difficulty finding people who knew even the most elementary bookkeeping or had heard of the most common business terms. At the time there were no business textbooks or business courses, so the transactional costs of making oneself understood were extremely high. Sixty years later, by 1950 or 1960, the large oil companies that succeeded the Standard Oil Trust could confidently assume that their more senior employees were business literate.

By now the new information technology—Internet and e-mail—have practically eliminated the physical costs of communications. This has meant that the most productive and most profitable way to organize is to disintegrate. This is being extended to more and more activities. Outsourcing the management of an institution's information technology, data processing, and computer system has become routine. In the early 1990s most American computer firms, e.g., Apple, even outsourced the production of their hardware to manufacturers in Japan or Singapore. In the late 1990s practically every Japanese consumer-electronics company repaid the compliment by outsourcing the manufacturing of its products for the American market to American contract manufacturers.

In the past few years the entire human-resources management of more than 2 million American workers—hiring, firing, training, benefits, and so on—has been outsourced to professional employee organizations. This sector, which ten years ago barely existed, is now growing 30 percent a year. It originally concentrated on small and medium-size companies, but the biggest of the firms, Exult, founded only in 1998, now manages employment issues for a number of Fortune 500 companies, including BP, a British-American oil giant, and Unisys, a computer maker. According to a study by McKinsey, a consultancy, outsourcing human-relations management in this way can save up to 30 percent of the cost and increase employee satisfaction as well.

4. The customer now has the information. As yet, the Internet lacks the equivalent of a telephone book that would make it easy for users to find what they are looking for. It still requires pecking and hunting. But the information is somewhere on a Web site, and search firms to find it for a fee are rapidly developing. Whoever has the information has the power. Power is thus shifting to the customer, be it another business or the ultimate consumer. Specifically, that means the supplier, e.g., the manufacturer, will cease to be a seller and instead become a buyer for the customer. This is already happening.

General Motors (GM), still the world's largest manufacturer and for many years its most successful selling organization, last year announced the creation of a major business that will buy for the ultimate car consumer. Although wholly owned by GM, the business will be autonomous and will buy not only General Motors cars, but whatever car and model most closely fits the individual customer's preferences, values, and wallet.

5. Lastly, there are few unique technologies anymore. Increasingly, the knowledge needed in a given industry comes out of some totally different technology with which, very often, the people in the industry are unfamiliar. No one in the telephone industry knew anything about fiberglass cables. They were developed by a glass company, Corning. Conversely, more than half the important inventions developed since the Second World War by the most productive of the great research labs, the Bell Laboratories, have been applied mainly outside the telephone industry.

The Bell Labs' most significant invention of the past fifty years was the transistor, which created the modern electronics industry. But the telephone company saw so little use for this revolutionary new device that it practically gave it away to anybody who asked for it—which is what put Sony, and with it the Japanese, into the consumer-electronics business.

Who Needs a Research Lab?

Research directors, as well as high-tech industrialists, now tend to believe that the company-owned research lab, that proud nineteenth-century invention, has become obsolete.

This explains why, increasingly, development and growth of a business are taking place not inside the corporation itself but through partnerships, joint ventures, alliances, minority participation, and know-how agreements with institutions in different industries and with a different technology. Something that only fifty years ago would have been unthinkable is becoming common: alliances between institutions of a totally different character, say a profit-making company and a university department, or a city or state government and a business that contracts for a specific service such as cleaning the streets or running prisons.

Practically no product or service any longer has either a single specific end-use or application, or its own market. Commercial paper competes with the banks' commercial loans. Cardboard, plastic, and aluminum compete with glass for the bottle market. Glass is replacing copper in cables. Steel is competing with wood and plastic in providing the studs around which the American one-family home is constructed. The deferred annuity is pushing aside traditional life insurance—but, in turn, insurance companies rather than financial service institutions are becoming the managers of commercial risks.

A "glass company" may therefore have to redefine itself by what it is good at doing rather than by the material in which it has specialized in the past. One of the world's largest glassmakers, Corning, sold its profitable business making traditional glass products to become the number one producer and supplier of high-tech materials. Merck,

America's largest pharmaceutical company, diversified from making drugs into wholesaling every kind of pharmacy product, most of them not even made by Merck, and a good many by competitors.

The same sort of thing is happening in the nonbusiness sectors of the economy. One example is the freestanding "birthing center" run by a group of obstetricians that competes with the American hospital's maternity ward. And Britain, long before the Internet, created the "open university," which allows people to get a university education and obtain a degree without ever setting foot in a classroom or attending a lecture.

The Next Company

One thing is almost certain: In future there will be not one kind of corporation but several different ones. The modern company was invented simultaneously but independently in three countries: America, Germany, and Japan. It was a complete novelty and bore no resemblance to the economic organization that had been the "economic enterprise" for millennia: the small, privately owned, and personally run firm. As late as 1832, England's *McLane Report*—the first statistical survey of business—found that nearly all firms were privately owned and had fewer than ten employees. The only exceptions were quasi-governmental organizations such as the Bank of England or the East India Company. Forty years later a new kind of organization with thousands of employees had appeared on the scene, e.g., the American railroads, built with federal and state support, and Germany's Deutsche Bank.

Wherever the corporation went, it acquired some national characteristics and adapted to different legal rules in each country. Moreover, very large corporations everywhere are being run quite differently from the small owner-managed kind. And there are substantial internal differences in culture, values, and rhetoric between corporations in different industries. Banks everywhere are very much alike, and so are retailers or manufacturers. But banks everywhere are different from retailers or manufacturers. Otherwise, however, the differences between corporations everywhere are more of style than of substance. The same is true of all other organizations in modern society: government agencies, armed forces, hospitals, universities, and so on.

The tide turned around 1970, first with the emergence of new institutional investors such as pension funds and mutual trusts as the new owners, then—more decisively— with the emergence of knowledge workers as the economy's big new resource and the society's representative class. The result has been a fundamental change in the corporation.

A bank in the Next Society will still not look like a hospital nor be run like one. But different banks may be quite different from one another, depending on how each of them responds to the changes in its workforce, technology, and markets. A number of different models are likely to emerge, especially of organization and structure, but perhaps also of recognitions and rewards.

The same legal entity—e.g., a business, a government agency, or a large not-for-profit organization—may well contain several different human organizations that inter-lock, but are managed separately and differently. One of these is likely to be a traditional organization of full-time employees. Yet there may also be a closely linked but separately managed human organization made up mainly of older people who are not employees but associates or affiliates. And there are likely to be "perimeter" groups such as the people who work for the organization, even full-time, but as employees of an outsourcing contractor or of a contract manufacturer. These people have no con-tractual relationship with the business they work for, which in turn has no control over them. They may not have to be "managed," but they have to be made produc-tive. They will therefore have to be deployed where their specialized knowledge can make the greatest contribution. Despite all the present talk of "knowledge management," no one yet really knows how to do it.

Just as important, the people in every one of these or-ganizational categories will have to be satisfied. Attracting them and holding them will become the central task of people management. We already know what does not work: bribery. In the past ten or fifteen years many busi-nesses in America have used bonuses or stock options to attract and keep knowledge workers. It always fails.

According to an old saying, you cannot hire a hand,

the whole man always comes with it. But you cannot hire a man either; the spouse almost always comes with it. And the spouse has already spent the money when falling profits eliminate the bonus or falling stock prices make the option worthless. Then both the employee and the spouse feel bitter and betrayed.

Of course knowledge workers need to be satisfied with their pay, because dissatisfaction with income and benefits is a powerful disincentive. The incentives, however, are different. The management of knowledge workers should be based on the assumption that the corporation needs them more than they need the corporation. They know they can leave. They have both mobility and self-confidence. This means they have to be treated and managed as volunteers, in the same way as volunteers who work for not-for-profit organizations. The first thing such people want to know is what the company is trying to do and where it is going. Next, they are interested in personal achievement and personal responsibility—which means they have to be put in the right job. Knowledge workers expect continuous learning and continuous training. Above all, they want respect, not so much for themselves but for their area of knowledge. In that regard, they have moved several steps beyond traditional workers, who used to expect to be told what to do, although lately they are increasingly expected to "participate." Knowledge workers, by contrast, expect to make the decisions in their own area.

From Corporation to Confederation

Eighty years ago, GM first developed both the organizational concepts and the organizational structure on which today's large corporations everywhere are based. It also invented the idea of a distinct top management. Now it is experimenting with a range of new organizational models. It has been changing itself from a unitary corporation held together by control through ownership into a group held together by management control, with GM often holding only a minority stake. GM now controls but does not own Fiat, itself one of the oldest and largest carmakers. It also controls Saab in Sweden and two smaller Japanese carmakers, Suzuki and Isuzu.

At the same time GM has divested itself of much of its manufacturing by spinning off into a separate company, called Delphi, the making of parts and accessories that together account for 60–70 percent of the cost of producing a car. Instead of owning—or at least controlling—the suppliers of parts and accessories, GM will in future buy them at auction and on the Internet. It has joined up with its American competitors Ford and DaimlerChrysler to create an independent purchasing cooperative that will buy for its members from whatever source offers the best deal. All the other carmakers have been invited to join.

GM will still design its cars, it will still make engines, and it will still assemble. It will also still sell its cars through its dealer network. But in addition to selling its

283

own cars, GM intends to become a car merchant and a buyer for the ultimate consumer, finding the right car for the buyer no matter who makes it.

The Toyota Way

GM is still the world's largest car manufacturer, but for the past twenty years Toyota has been the most successful one. Like GM, Toyota is building a worldwide group, but unlike GM, Toyota has organized its group round its core competence in manufacturing. The company is moving away from having multiple suppliers of parts and accessories, ultimately aiming for no more than two suppliers for any one part. These suppliers will be separate and independent companies, owned locally, but Toyota will in effect run their manufacturing operation for them. They will get the Toyota business only if they agree to being inspected and "advised" by a special Toyota manufacturing consulting organization. And Toyota will also do most of the design work for the suppliers.

This is not a new idea. Sears Roebuck did the same for its suppliers in the 1920s and 1930s. Britain's Marks & Spencer, although in deep trouble now, was the world's most successful retailer for fifty years, maintaining its preeminence largely by keeping an iron grip on its suppliers. It is rumored in Japan that Toyota intends ultimately to market its manufacturing consultancy to noncar companies, turning its manufacturing core competence into a separate big business.

Yet another approach is being explored by a large manufacturer of branded and packaged consumer goods. Some 60 percent of the company's products are sold in the developed countries through some 150 retail chains. The company plans to create a worldwide Web site that will take orders direct from customers in all countries, either to be picked up in the retail store nearest to them or to be delivered by that store to their home. But—and this is the true innovation—the Web site will also take orders for noncompeting packaged and branded consumer products made by other, and especially smaller, firms. Such firms have great difficulty in getting their wares onto increasingly crowded supermarket shelves. The multinational's Web site could offer them direct access to customers and delivery through an established large retailer. The payoff for the multinational and the retailer would be that both get a decent commission without having to invest any money of their own, without risk and without sacrificing shelf space to slow-moving items.

There are already a good many variations on this theme: the American contract manufacturers, already mentioned, who now make the products for half a dozen competing Japanese consumer-electronics firms; a few independent specialists who design software for competing information-hardware makers; the independent specialists who design credit cards for competing American banks and also often market and clear the cards for the bank. All the bank does is the financing.

These approaches, however different, still all take the traditional corporation as their point of departure. But there are also some new ideas that do away with the corporate model altogether. One example is a "syndicate" being tested by several noncompeting manufacturers in the European Union. Each of the constituent companies is medium-size, family-owned, and owner-managed. Each is a leader in a narrow, highly engineered product line. Each is heavily export-dependent. The individual companies intend to remain independent, and to continue to design their products separately. They will also continue to make them in their own plants for their main markets, and to sell them in these markets. But for other markets, and especially for emerging or less developed countries, the syndicate will arrange for the making of the products, either in syndicate-owned plants producing for several of the members or by local contract manufacturers. The syndicate will handle the delivery of all members' products and service them in all markets. Each member will own a share of the syndicate, and the syndicate, in turn, will own a small share of each member's capital. If this sounds familiar, it is. The model is the nineteenth-century farmers' cooperative.

◆ *The Future of Top Management*

As the corporation moves toward a confederation or a syndicate, it will increasingly need a top management that is separate, powerful, and accountable. This top management's responsibilities will cover the entire organization's direction, planning, strategy, values, and principles; its structure and its relationship between its various members; its alliances, partnerships, and joint ventures; and its research, design, and innovation. It will have to take charge of the management of the two resources common to all units of the organization: key people and money. It will represent the corporation to the outside world and maintain relationships with governments, the public, the media, and organized labor.

Life at the Top

An equally important task for top management in the Next Society's corporation will be to balance the three dimensions of the corporation: as an economic organization, as a human organization, and as an increasingly important social organization. Each of the three models of the corporation developed in the past half-century stressed one of these dimensions and subordinated the other two. The German model of the "social market economy" put the emphasis on the social dimension, the Japanese one on the human dimension, and the American one ("shareholder sovereignty") on the economic dimension.

None of the three is adequate on its own. The German model achieved both economic success and social stability, but at the price of high unemployment and dangerous labor-market rigidity. The Japanese model was strikingly successful for twenty years, but faltered at the first serious challenge; indeed it has become a major obstacle to recovery from Japan's present recession. Shareholder sovereignty is also bound to flounder. It is a fair-weather model that works well only in times of prosperity. Obviously the enterprise can fulfill its human and social functions only if it prospers as a business. But now that knowledge workers are becoming the key employees, a company also needs to be a desirable employer to be successful.

Paradoxically, the claim to the absolute primacy of business gains that made shareholder sovereignty possible has also highlighted the importance of the corporation's social function. The new shareholders whose emergence since 1960 or 1970 produced shareholder sovereignty are not "capitalists." They are employees who own a stake in the business through their retirement and pension funds. By 2000, pension funds and mutual funds had come to own the majority of the share capital of America's large companies. This has given shareholders the power to demand short-term rewards. But the need for a secure retirement income will increasingly focus on people's minds on the future value of the investment. Corporations, therefore, will have to pay attention both to their short-term business results and to their long-term performance as providers of retirement benefits. The two are not irreconcilable, but they are different, and they will have to be balanced.

Over the past decade or two, managing a large corporation has changed out of all recognition. That explains the emergence of the "CEO superman," such as Jack Welch of GE, Andrew Grove of Intel, or Sanford Weill of Citigroup. But organizations cannot rely on supermen to run them; the supply is both unpredictable and far too limited. Organizations survive only if they can be run by competent people who take their job seriously. That it takes genius today to be the boss of a big organization clearly indicates that top management is in crisis.

Impossible Jobs

The recent failure rate of chief executives in big American companies points in the same direction. A large proportion of CEOs of such companies appointed in the past ten years were fired as failures within a year or two. But each of these people had been picked for his proven competence, and each had been highly successful in his previous jobs. This suggests that the jobs they took on had become undoable. The American record suggests not human failure but systems failure. Top management in big organizations needs a new concept.

Some elements of such a concept are beginning to emerge. For instance, Jack Welch at GE has built a top-management team in which the company's chief financial officer and its chief human-resources officer are near equals to the chief executive and are both excluded from the succession to the top job. He has also given himself and his team a clear and publicly announced priority task on which to concentrate. During his twenty years in the top job, Mr. Welch has had three such priorities, each occupying him for five years or more. Each time he has delegated everything else to the top managements of the operating businesses within the GE confederation.

A different approach has been taken by Asea Brown Boveri (ABB), a huge Swedish-Swiss engineering multinational. Goran Lindahl, who retired as chief executive earlier this year, went even further than GE in making the individual units within the company into separate worldwide businesses and building up a strong top-management team of a few nonoperating people. But he also defined for himself a new role as a one-man information system for the company, traveling incessantly to get to know all the senior managers personally, listening to them and telling them what went on within the organization.

A largish financial services company tried another idea: appointing not one CEO but six. The head of each of the five operating businesses is also CEO for the whole company in one top-management area, such as corporate planning and strategy or human resources. The company's chairman represents the company to the outside world and is also directly concerned with obtaining, allocating, and managing capital. All six people meet twice a week as the top management committee. This seems to work well, but only because none of the five operating CEOs wants the chairman's job; each prefers to stay in operations. Even the man who designed the system, and then himself took the chairman's job, doubts that the system will survive once he is gone.

In their different ways, the top people at all of these companies were trying to do the same thing: to establish their organization's unique personality. And that may well be the most important task for top management in the Next Society's big organizations. In the half-century after the Second World War, the business corporation has brilliantly proved itself as an economic organization, i.e., a creator of wealth and jobs. In the Next Society, the biggest challenge for the large company—especially for the multinational—may be its social legitimacy: its values, its mission, its vision. Increasingly, in the Next Society's corporation, top management will, in fact, be the company. Everything else can be outsourced.

Will the corporation survive? Yes, after a fashion. Something akin to a corporation will have to coordinate the Next Society's economic resources. Legally and perhaps financially, it may even look much the same as today's corporation. But instead of there being a single model adopted by everyone, there will be a range of models to choose from. And there equally will be a number of top-management models to choose from.

◆ *The Way Ahead*

The Next Society has not quite arrived yet, but it has got far enough for action to be considered in the following areas:

The Future Corporation

Enterprises—including a good many nonbusinesses, such as universities—should start experimenting with new corporate forms and conducting a few pilot studies, especially in working with alliances, partners, and joint ventures, and in defining new structures and new tasks for top management. New models are also needed for geographical and product diversification for multinational companies, and for balancing concentration and diversification.

People Policies

The way people are managed almost everywhere assumes that the workforce is still largely made up of people who are employed by the enterprise and work full-time for it until they are fired, quit, retire, or die. Yet already in many organizations as many as two-fifths of the people who work there are not employees and do not work full-time.

Today's human-resources managers also still assume that the most desirable and least costly employees are young ones. In America especially, older people, and particularly older managers and professionals, have been pushed into early retirement to make room for younger people, who are believed to cost less or to have more up-to-date skills. The results of this policy have not been encouraging. Generally speaking, after two years wage costs per employee for the younger recruits tend to be back where they were before the "oldies" were pushed out, if not higher. The number of salaried employees seems to be going up at least as fast as production or sales, which means that the new young hires are no more productive than the old ones were. But in any event, demography will make the present policy increasingly self-defeating and expensive.

The first need is for a people policy that covers all those who work for an enterprise, whether they are employed by it or not. After all, the performance of every single one of them matters. So far, no one seems to have devised a satisfactory solution to this problem. Second, enterprises must attract, hold, and make productive people who have reached official retirement age, have become independent outside contractors, or are not available as full-time permanent employees. For example, highly skilled and educated older people, instead of being retired, might be offered a choice of continuing relationships that convert them into long-term "inside outsiders," preserving their skill and knowledge for the enterprise and yet giving them the flexibility and freedom they expect and can afford.

There is a model for this, but it comes from academia rather than business: the professor emeritus, who has vacated his chair and no longer draws a salary. He remains free to teach as much as he wants, but gets paid only for what he does. Many emeriti do retire altogether, but perhaps as many as half continue to teach part-time, and many continue to do full-time research. A similar arrangement might well suit senior professionals in a business. A big American corporation is currently trying out such an arrangement for older top-level people in its law and tax departments, in research and development, and in staff jobs. But for people in operating work, e.g., sales or manufacturing, something different needs to be developed.

Outside Information

Perhaps surprisingly, it can be argued that the Information Revolution has caused managements to be less well informed than they were before. They have more data, to be sure, but most of the information so readily made available by IT is about internal company matters. As this survey has shown, though, the most important changes affecting an institution today are likely to be outside ones, which present information systems usually know nothing about.

One reason is that information about the outside world is rarely available in computer-usable form. It is not codified, nor is it usually quantified. This is why IT people, and their executive customers, tend to scorn information about the outside world as "anecdotal." Moreover, far too many managers assume, wrongly, that the society they have known all their lives will remain the same forever.

Outside information is now becoming available on the Internet. Although this is still in totally disorganized form, it is now possible for managements to ask what outside information they need, as a first step toward devising a proper information system for collecting relevant information about the outside world.

Change Agents

To survive and succeed, every organization will have to turn itself into a change agent. The most effective way to manage change successfully is to create it. But experience has shown that grafting innovation on to a traditional enterprise does not work. The enterprise has to become a change agent. This requires the organized abandonment of things that have been shown to be unsuccessful, and the organized and continuous improvement of every product, service, and process within the enterprise (which the Japanese call *kaizen*). It requires the exploitation of successes, especially unexpected and unplanned-for ones, and it requires systematic innovation. The point of becoming a change agent is that it changes the mind-set of the entire organization. Instead of seeing change as a threat, its people will come to consider it an opportunity.

And Then?

So much for getting ready for the future that we can already see taking shape. But what about future trends and events we are not even aware of yet? If there is one thing that can be forecast with confidence, it is that the future will turn out in unexpected ways.

Take, for example, the Information Revolution. Almost everybody is sure of two things about it: first, that it is proceeding with unprecedented speed; and second, that its effects will be more radical than anything that has gone before. Wrong, and wrong again. Both in its speed and its impact, the Information Revolution uncannily resembles its two predecessors within the past two hundred years, the First Industrial Revolution of the later eighteenth and early nineteenth centuries and the Second Industrial Revolution in the late nineteenth century.

The First Industrial Revolution, triggered by James Watt's improved steam engine in the mid-1770s, immediately had an enormous impact on the West's imagination, but it did not produce many social and economic changes until the invention of the railroad in 1829, and of prepaid postal service and of the telegraph in the decade thereafter. Similarly, the invention of the computer in the mid-1940s, the Information Revolution's equivalent of the steam engine, stimulated people's imagination, but it was not until more than forty years later, with the spread of the Internet in the 1990s, that the Information Revolution began to bring about big economic and social changes.

Equally, today we are puzzled and alarmed by the growing inequality in income and wealth and by the emergence of the "superrich," such as Microsoft's Bill Gates. Yet the same sudden and inexplicable growth in inequality, and the same emergence of the "superrich" of their day, characterized both the First and the Second Industrial Revolutions. Relative to the average income and average wealth of their time and country, those earlier superrich were a good deal richer than a Bill Gates is relative to today's average income and wealth in America.

These parallels are close and striking enough to make it almost certain that, as in the earlier Industrial Revolutions, the main effects of the Information Revolution on the Next Society still lie ahead. The decades of the nineteenth century following the First and Second Industrial Revolutions were the most innovative and most fertile periods since the sixteenth century for the creation of new institutions and new theories. The First Industrial Revolution turned the factory into the central production organization and the main creator of wealth. Factory workers became the first new social class since the appearance of knights in armor more than one thousand years earlier. The house of Rothschild, which emerged as the world's dominant financial power after 1810, was not only the first investment bank but also the first multinational company since the fifteenth century Hanseatic League and the Medici. The First Industrial Revolution brought forth, among many other things, intellectual property, universal incorporation, limited liability, the trade union, the cooperative, the technical university, and the daily newspaper. The Second Industrial Revolution produced the modern civil service and the modern corporation, the commercial bank, the business school, and the first nonmenial jobs outside the home for women.

The two Industrial Revolutions also bred new theories and new ideologies. *The Communist Manifesto* was a response to the first Industrial Revolution; the political theories that together shaped the twentieth-century democracies—Bismarck's welfare state, Britain's Christian Socialism and Fabians, America's regulation of business— were all responses to the second one. So was Frederick Winslow Taylor's "scientific management" (starting in 1881), with its productivity explosion.

Big Ideas

Following the Information Revolution, once again we see the emergence of new institutions and new theories. The new economic regions—the European Union, NAFTA, and the proposed Free-Trade Area of the Americas—are neither traditionally free-trade nor traditionally protectionist. They attempt a new balance between the two, and between the economic sovereignty of the national state and supranational economic decision-making. Equally, there is no real precedent for the Citigroups, Goldman

Sachses, or ING Barings that have come to dominate world finance. They are not multinational but transnational. The money they deal in is almost totally beyond the control of any country's government or central bank.

And then there is the upsurge in interest in Joseph Schumpeter's postulates of "dynamic disequilibrium" as the economy's only stable state; of the innovator's "creative destruction" as the economy's driving force; and of new technology as the main, if not the only, economic change agent—the very antithesis of all prevailing economic theories based on the idea of equilibrium as a healthy economy's norm, monetary and fiscal policies as the drivers of a modern economy, and technology as an "externality."

All this suggests that the greatest changes are almost certainly still ahead of us. We can also be sure that the society of 2030 will be very different from that of today, and that it will bear little resemblance to that predicted by today's best-selling futurists. It will not be dominated or even shaped by information technology. IT will, of course, be important, but it will be only one of several important new technologies. The central feature of the Next Society, as of its predecessors, will be new institutions and new theories, ideologies, and problems.

(2001)

Acknowledgments

I always prepublish chapters of an essay volume such as this either as magazine articles or magazine interviews. This gives me professional editing by the editors of the magazines in which the pieces appear and by professional interviewers. It is "feedback" of a quality and insight I could not possibly attain any other way. It has only one slight drawback: The figures and statistics in each piece are those of the year in which it was prepublished rather than those of the year in which it appears as a chapter in this book. To update them could, however, only create confusion. And in no case has there been a change in the trends that these figures illustrate. Hence (as already said in the preface) it appeared preferable to my publisher and to me not to update these figures and statistics, but, rather, to indicate in the book when the individual chapter was first published—which also enables readers to judge for themselves whether I rightly diagnosed developments or whether subsequent events have invalidated my thesis. And, together with my publisher, I decided not to change anything in any chapter except to correct typographical and spelling errors, and, in some cases, to change the title (usually by replacing the title an individual publication's editor chose with my original title for the piece). Otherwise each chapter appears as it was first written. And anyhow, the latest available figures—those for 2000 and 2001—are to be found here in the most recently published sections, especially in Part IV.

More than a fifth of this book was first published by *The Economist* (London): chapter 4 ("E-Commerce: The Central Challenge") in the *Economist Yearbook* for the year 2000; chapter 9 ("Financial Services: Innovate or Die") in the magazine itself in the year 1999; and chapter 15, the entire final part ("The Next Society"), as an *Economist Survey* in late fall 2001. Four chapters were prepublished as interviews: chapter 2 ("The Exploding World of the Internet") in *Red Herring,* 2001; chapter 5 ("The New Economy Isn't Here Yet") in *Business 2.0,* 2000; chapter 7 ("Entrepreneurs and Innovation") in *Inc. Magazine,* 1996; chapter 10 ("Moving Beyond Capitalism?") in *New Perspectives,* 1998. Two chapters—chapters 12 ("The Global Economy and the Nation-State") and 13 ("It's the Society, Stupid")—were prepublished in *Foreign Affairs* (respectively in 1997 and 1998). And one chapter each was prepublished in *Viewpoint* (chapter 6: "The CEO in the New Millennium," 1997); in *Forbes/ASAP* (chapter 3: "From Computer Literacy to Information Literacy," 1998); in *Leader to Leader* (chapter 14: "On Civilizing the City," 1998); in *Atlantic Monthly* (chapter 1: "Beyond the Information Revolution," 1999); in the *Wall Street Journal* (chapter 11: "The Rise of the Great Institutions," 1999); and in the *Harvard Business Review* (chapter 8: "They're Not Employees, They're People," 2002). I want to express my gratitude to the editors of these publications and to the four interviewers for their questions, their criticism, their editorial changes, and recommendations.

And, as with earlier essay volumes of mine, this one owes an enormous debt to my long-term publisher, Truman M. Talley of Truman Talley Books. He has been my guide and my counselor in choosing the topics and in working out the book's final structure. My readers and I owe him profound thanks.

Index

Index

Index

Index

magazines, 14, 59
Mahathir, Mohamad, 163
Malaysia, 163
managed care, 34
management, American, 95
management base, outgrowing, 99–101
management consultants, 86
management levels, 47–48, 68
management team, building, 101–2
managers
  huge profits of, 64, 150
  top level, 241, 287–90
manual workers, 33–34, 129, 252–53
Manufacturers Bank, 134
manufacturing
  accounting for, 52
  decline of, x, 240
  new practices, 264–65
  productivity and income share of, 73–74, 240, 263–67
  protectionism in, 268–69
manufacturing companies, 36–38
  survival of, 77
manufacturing workers, 40, 252, 269–70
Mao Tse Tung, 32
maquiladoras, 117
market forces, 32
markets
  global, 196–98
  mass, 144, 237, 246–47

unexpected, 96–98
unstable, 27, 152
market share, 37, 64
Marks & Spencer, 284
Marshall, George, 200
Marshall Plan, 199–200
Marx, Karl, 38, 183
mass markets, 237, 246–47
mass production, 6
Matsushita, 94
Maxwell, James Clerk, 21
McCormick, Cyrus, 104
McKinsey & Co., 115, 197
McLuhan, Marshall, 31
meals on wheels, 157
medical technologists, 256
mental geography, 9, 12–13
Merck, 95, 278–79
Mercosur, 240, 269
mergers, 135
Merrill Lynch, 134, 138, 147, 219–20
message, 47
Mexico, 39, 117, 188, 189, 268
microchips, price of, 5
Microsoft, 26, 60, 154, 171
  antitrust trial, 72
middle class, aging, affluent, 143–44
Mideast, xiii
military, 210, 212–13
millionaires, 23
mind-share, 64
Mitterand, François, 188
Mohn, Reinhard, 95

Index

Socrates, 68
software, 22–23
    advances in, 10
Sony, 94, 123, 277
Soros, George, 149
South Korea, 267
Spain, 243
specialization, 118–22, 259
speculation, 10, 15, 64–65, 208–
    9, 217, 247
speech therapists, 259
Standard Oil, 72, 272, 275
start-ups, 64–65
steamboat, 8, 13
steam engine, 5, 16
steam turbine, 16
steel industry, 104, 263, 272
stock market
    booms, 23, 25
    newsletters, 99
    speculators, 10, 15
stock market valuation, 26–27,
    65, 66–67
stock options, 25, 27–28, 281–82
strikes, 179
students, 31–32
subsidies, 38–39, 265, 268–69,
    270–71
success, rejecting, 97–98
Suharto, 163–64
Sumitomo, 137
supermarkets, 13–14
supply and demand, 151
surgery, 83, 259
Suzuki, 283
Sweden, 188, 243

Switzerland, 188
symphony orchestra, 125
syndicates, 286

Taiwan, 94, 164, 267
taxes, 58, 176, 184, 249
Taylor, Frederick Winslow, 124,
    298
teachers, 31–32, 255
teachers unions, 31–32
technological changes, xi–xii, 4–
    11, 85
technologists, 20–22, 67
technology, 50
    transfer of, 88, 272–73, 277
technology companies, 26
telegraph, 16
telephone industry, 277
telephones, 43, 227–28
temp firms, 111–23
temp workers, 236, 249
    advantages of using, 114–23
    productivity of, 122–23
Tenneco Automotive, 113
terrorism, xii–xiii
Texaco, 72
textiles
    factory manufacture, 5–7
    price of, 5
Thailand, 268
third-world countries, 32
Thucydides, 72
Tocqueville, Alexis de, 211
Toennies, Ferdinand, 229–30
Total Quality Management, 124
tourism, 194

Index

Index

Weber, Max, 214
Weill, Sanford, 289
Welch, Jack, 74, 289, 290
welfare mothers, 158
welfare state, 160
Westinghouse, 126
Whitney, Eli, 6, 21
women, working, 248–49, 255–56
workforce
    categories of, 118, 214, 252–71
    managing, 123
    productivity of, 124–25, 194
    specialization of, 118–22
    training, 253
    young vs. old, 248–51
working class, 6
workmen's compensation, 33–34
workweek, 171

World Trade Organization, 245
World War I, 199, 200, 210, 212
World War II, 87, 94, 194, 199–200, 210
Wriston, Walter, 140

Yamaha, 94
Yamaichi, 137, 138, 219–20
young people, 35–36, 171–72
    decreased numbers of, 235–37
    employees, 235–37
youth culture, 36
youth market, 237, 247–48
Yugoslavia, 184

zero-sum game, 138
zipper, 69